HOW TO BECOME
A SUCCESSFUL
WEEKEND
ENTREPRENEUR

How to Order:

Single copies may be ordered from Prima Publishing, P.O. Box 1260BK, Rocklin, CA 95677; telephone (916) 786-0426. Quantity discounts are also available. On your letterhead, include information concerning the intended use of the books and the number of books you wish to purchase.

HOW TO BECOME A SUCCESSFUL WEEKEND ENTREPRENEUR

Secrets of Making an Extra $100 <u>or More</u> Each Week Using Your Spare Time

Jennifer Basye

Prima Publishing
P.O. Box 1260BK
Rocklin, CA 95677
(916) 786-0426

Production: Robin Lockwood, Bookman Productions
Copyediting: Lura Harrison and Carol Ann Sheffield
Composition: Janet Hansen, Alphatype
Interior design: Judith Levinson
Cover design: The Dunlavey Studio, Sacramento

Library of Congress Cataloging-in-Publication Data

Basye, Jennifer.
How to become a successful weekend entrepreneur / Jennifer Basye.
     p.   cm.
    ISBN 1-55958-288-X
    1. Supplementary employment. 2. New business enterprises.
    3. Entrepreneurship.   I. Title.
HD5854.5.B39   1993
658.4'21—dc20   92-40478
                                       CIP

94 95 96 97 98 RRD 10 9 8 7 6 5 4 3 2 1

Printed in the United States of America

ACKNOWLEDGMENTS

Many people have helped in the development of *How to Become a Successful Weekend Entrepreneur,* and I would like to thank them all publicly. For everyone at Prima Publishing, from Ben and Nancy Dominitz on through all of the departments, thanks for your encouragement and enthusiasm. My husband, Peter Sander, has been a terrific partner throughout this project and has helped to write many of the Back to Basics business ideas. I have a wonderful group of friends and family who read the manuscript in varying stages of development and helped with suggestions, criticism, and new ideas— Anne Basye, Karen Blanco, Andi Reese Brady, Laura Lewis, and Barbara Curtis. And I would like to thank the huge group of folks across the country who took the time to talk to me about their weekend entrepreneurial experiences and share their knowledge with other fledgling weekend entrepreneurs. In no particular order (certainly not alphabetical!) they are: Sherry Miller, Chris Trujillo, Darcy Tietjen, Dan Newey, Dusty Smale, Margaret Cable, Jerry Greenberg, The Amneus Family, Rhonda Jurkowski, Christl Saed, Cathleen Swanson, Mark Miyamoto, Donna Bates, Jerry Becker, the folks at Sacramento Beekeeping, Nancy Leneis, Lisa Monckton, Mimi Luebbermann, Bill Senecal and the staff at Beers Books, John Hall, Lee Strudivant, Danuta Lake, Ag Access bookstore, Kristine Backus, Shirley Shames, Jaydine Randall, Scott Standfil, Don Ballard, Elizabeth and Ian McPhail, Shirley Fong-Torres, Frances Hamilton, Maggie Lee, Christie McKinnon, Wanda Adelsberger, Brian Burch, Chris Dominguez, Dean Handy, Todd Walton and everyone in my writing group, Julie Didion, Lewis Buzbee, Mary Charles, Sandy Hoover, Kathy Lee, Scott Bobo, Maia Amos, the Sierra Club Store in Sacramento, Eleanor Nathan, Sarah Buck, Diane Howe, Mindy Toomay, Susann Geiskopf-Hadler, Elaine Corn, Martha Casselman, Kathy Smith, Mark Sedgley, Travis Boersma, the Mortenson family, Karen Jackson, James Meek, Debra Lilly, Jim Goodykoontz, Bettie Renda, George Bingham, Mike Ingram,

Gina Lewis, Arik Trebnik, Lisa Soderborg, Cindy Davis, Stacey Ball, my brothers John and Paul Basye, and, of course, my very own Mom and Dad—Mary Alice and George Basye. My mother plans to publish a rebuttal soon; she worries that this book makes it look as though they turned me out onto the streets at an early age to sell matches.

CONTENTS

INTRODUCTION

After a long week of work for a book publishing company, I get up bright and early every Saturday morning and go to the headquarters of my own company (by crossing the hall into the spare bedroom). For two hours every week I run my own teeny-tiny one-book publishing company, and in that time I make anywhere from $100–$300, depending on how heavy my mail has been. I spend my two hours opening orders, addressing and filling envelopes with copies of my self-published travel book *The Air Courier's Handbook,* answering mail from readers, endorsing checks, and to top it off I treat myself and my dog with a quick walk to the bank to make the weekly deposit. Sweet Leilani and I enjoy that part most of all.

Once my weekly publishing business is handled, I turn my attention to my other entrepreneurial job. Classical music from the CD player fills the air as I work at the dining room table making hand rolled beeswax candles to sell at a Sunday crafts fair. In an hour I produce enough to sell throughout a busy afternoon. Putting my craft supplies away, I decide to spend the rest of Saturday bicycling with my husband. Ah, but I love the life of a weekend entrepreneur!

Bookstore shelves are filled with home-based business books of every description, each one promising that you can successfully quit your job and support yourself and your family with a business of your very own. In today's tricky economy that is a risk that fewer and fewer of us are willing to make. Better to hang on to the secure job that you have now and use your *free time* to generate that much needed second income. (And if the unthinkable happens, and you someday lose your fulltime job, you will be in a much better cash position until you find another.) Weekends, evenings, and even quiet early morning hours can be turned into a new-found cash machine of your very own as you become a *Weekend Entrepreneur!*

Within the pages of this book, you will find business ideas of every description that require little or no experience to achieve success (just hard work and dedication). There are ten chapters filled with solid ideas to choose from, ideas which have been put into action by folks just like you. Many of the business ideas include real-life advice and stories from the actual weekend entrepreneurs who have made them work. I'm certain that there is an idea here that will work for you. If after reading this book you can't find a business idea that suits you, just send me a short description of what you have done in your life along with a self-addressed, stamped envelope, and I will send you a personal letter of entrepreneurial advice, *no charge*. (See my business address at the end of this introduction.)

Remember, there is no sense working a second job at a fast food joint to meet the bills or buy those extra treats for yourself and your family when you can get started this weekend as a part-time entrepreneur working as much as you want. Your future rests in your very own hands, go out and make it happen. Buying a book about weekend entrepreneurs is a good first step, but it takes courage to take the next few steps toward success. If one idea doesn't seem to work for you, instead of giving up, please try another.

Good luck, and let me hear about your success so that I can include *you* and *your business* in a future edition of this book!

Jennifer Basye
Prima Publishing
1830 Sierra Gardens, Ste. 130
Roseville, CA 95661

Chapter One

The Weekend Entrepreneur

I have been a weekend entrepreneur ever since I was tall enough to slide a bank deposit over the counter to the teller. As a small child I baked cherry pie after cherry pie for my grandfather to give as gifts to his patients. Few jobs have paid as well since! I created sequinned jewelry as an enterprising teen, and started a small campus news bulletin while in college. Since graduating I have spent the work week happily employed in the book business, but I have never given up the thrill, the freedom, and the big financial rewards of working for myself on the weekends.

What is a weekend entrepreneur, you ask? A weekend entrepreneur is a hardworking and dedicated person who works as a salaried or hourly wage employee for someone else, but enjoys the benefits of creating more money in their spare time by working for themselves. The growing ranks of weekend entrepreneurs also include moms who have chosen to stay home with their small children, energetic teenagers looking for ways to earn a little spending money or start a savings account, college students who need a way to stretch their tuition loans, and retired folks who just aren't ready to stay away from the business world for good. Perhaps you are an office worker in the employ of a major corporation. Sure, you like your job but you would also enjoy a larger paycheck. This year's prospects for a raise look bleak for everyone, but what will you tell your son when he asks about summer camp? How can you tell your daughter that the budget is too tight for ballet lessons? And what if one of the kids needs braces? How can you meet your New Year's resolution to pay your credit cards off faster and end this year debt free?

What you need is a SAM—a Source of Additional Money! Start working for yourself as a weekend entrepreneur with a creative SAM and reward yourself with a more secure financial future!

Even people who make a top salary enjoy the freedom and excitement of having a weekend business. Perhaps you don't have to worry about meeting your basic bills, but wouldn't it be nice to have the extra money for a trip to Hawaii this year instead of just a long weekend in your own state?

Anyone can become a weekend entrepreneur. All across the country people just like you—accountants, truck drivers, sales clerks, construction workers, clergy, lawyers, teachers, students, and others from all walks of life—are choosing to add to their bank accounts by working part time for themselves. You work hard all week long in your regular job—why add to the stress by taking a second job working for another company? Take your time and your financial destiny into your own hands now and work as much or as little as you like. After all, you're the boss! Another plus to being a weekend entrepreneur is that with most of these business ideas you can stop it and start it again according to your cash needs. Of course, when that extra money starts coming in you won't want it to stop!

Not every type of business is suited to the needs of a weekend entrepreneur. The business ideas outlined here are specially chosen to suit part-time work, with a minimum of investment, experience, and overhead. For most of these businesses you will not need an office, just a spare corner of your house or apartment. I trust you, the reader, to investigate your local business laws and regulations and make certain that you follow them closely. This is important, as weekend entrepreneurs owe it to each other to follow the letter of the law in order not to give the profession a bad name. I also trust you to report your extra income in your annual tax return. Please consult a tax planner if you are not certain how to do this. Honest people sleep easier at night. Remember to be good to your customers and deliver 110% of what you have promised; happy customers are always your best (and least expensive!) advertisement.

Opportunities and Our Changing Lifestyles

While investigating weekend entrepreneurial opportunities around the country, I have stumbled across an interesting development in our society that I believe holds the key to success for many of us. Our lifestyles are changing rapidly and four distinct types of people seem to be emerging:

1. Due to the stagnant business economy, there are large numbers of employed people whose incomes have leveled off while their bills have grown. These people have a real need for a SAM—a Source of Additional Money!

2. And then there are the relatively successful folks who also enjoy a SAM to help them do a few extra things in life, like buy fancy camping equipment or enjoy weekly dinners at their favorite restaurant.

3. There is a group of working people who are so caught up in their careers that they have little or no time to take care of the basic things in life like cooking, cleaning, and running errands. What little free time they do have is spent relaxing, traveling, or pursuing their hobbies. These folks just don't want to deal with the mess that projects around the house can create—they want to skip the sweat and frustration of certain types of jobs.

4. An ever increasing segment of the American population is "silvering," a popular advertising term for growing old. As we age, sometimes we are less able to do the simple things in life that we have taken for granted all these years—drive a car to the grocery store, keep our windows shiny and clean, or weed the vegetable garden.

The financial needs of the first two groups—the group whose incomes have leveled off and the group who wants a few more of life's extras—can be met by designing businesses and services that cater to the needs of the other two groups. And the wonderful secret is that as the years pass, their needs will not diminish, but only increase! Here is a perfect built-in market for weekend entrepreneurs.

Looking to the Past

Among the ideas that follow for weekend entrepreneurs you will find some that are simple, old-fashioned, uncomplicated businesses and services that *used to exist* years ago but seem to have disappeared. This is another key to success as a weekend entrepreneur—look to the past for ideas that have fallen by the wayside in today's complicated world. It is perhaps too late to revive the role of the colorful countryside tinker traveling from town to town to fix cooking pots, but there are many other great ideas out there.

A successful business person is always on the lookout for new ideas and ways to take advantage of trends. Always watch for what's hot and find a way to make money from it. Buzzwords nowadays are "green" (environmentally sensitive), and "New Age." Who knows what will emerge in the coming years as the next trend? I have included a few ideas that fit in with these current trends, but there are doubtless many more out there to be developed.

Two brothers in Oregon spotted a growing trend—gourmet coffees—and fashioned a weekend business running a small espresso stand in the corner of a grocery store parking lot. Yes, it is an adult version of a lemonade stand, but it sure does attract the customers! Look for their success story in the Chapter 8, "Cooking Up Dollars," and also look for a related idea to help you capitalize on the gourmet coffee trend under the heading of *Home Coffee Delivery*. Keep your eyes, ears, and even taste buds open in order to be able to spot trends and capitalize on them as they are emerging. I recommend paying close attention to the stories in magazines, newspapers, and on television, you just never know when the right idea will present itself to you.

A Look at What's Inside

To help you find a weekend business that suits you, the next chapters are filled with business ideas that have been grouped in several different ways. These chapters include:

Back to Basics—Elbow Grease and a Strong Back

Among the best SAMs suited to weekend entrepreneurs are those requiring a strong back and a steady hand with a hammer and a willingness to get their hands dirty. Throughout history men and women have always been able to rely on labor to produce financial rewards, and it is just as true today. Fortunately, wages have risen since the days of feudalism! Handy work, repairs, and odd jobs are businesses that are quick-to-start, pay cash, and customers can frequently be found in your own neighborhood. This chapter details businesses for the handy person to choose from.

Old-Fashioned Money—Look to the Past for Your Financial Future

There are many plain old tried-and-true ways to make extra money on the weekends, and they can still work for you! Garage and yard sales, small farming projects like herb gardens and cut flowers, and the centuries-old tradition of beekeeping to name just a few, but in this chapter you will also find many other inventive ways to use tested money-making methods to your advantage. This chapter also includes business ideas for services that used to exist (like basic delivery services); they are needed more than ever in this fast-paced world.

Teen Stuff—Ten Cool Ways to Earn Cool Cash

Don't let your kids sit around and envy their friends for the cool stuff and extra spending money they might have, inspire them to get out and make some money of their own! It will relieve some of your cash-stress, build self-confidence and self-esteem, and keep them out of trouble. This chapter lists many ideal projects and entrepreneurial undertakings that are perfect for teenagers with enthusiasm and drive. Kids can start their college fund off with these terrific SAMs.

Crafty Business—Money-Making Ideas for Craft Fairs

Always doing something with your hands? Turn your hobby into a money machine with these ideas for profitable crafts projects. Learn how to turn hand-rolled beeswax candles into cash, fashion trendy chile wreathes for year-round sales, and paint dried gourds. Selling handmade items at craft fairs and bazaars can not only be a steady SAM, but a great deal of fun for the whole family to boot!

Odds and Ends—Great SAMs That Defy Categories!

These ideas just don't fit anywhere else! Perhaps your skills and interest also defy categories, and if so this is the chapter for you. Here are another ten SAMs that range from the wild to the weird (leading tours of graveyards?), but all are wonderfully fun moneymakers.

Available Talent—Opportunities for Artists and Musicians

For those of you lucky enough to be gifted with either artistic or musical talent, there are many opportunities available for hardworking weekend entrepreneurs. Face painting for children is a great way to use artistic skills, custom-made stationery is another. These businesses are carefully explained in this chapter, along with many other ways for talented folks to earn extra cash.

Cooking Up Dollars—Making Money in the Kitchen

Come the weekends, we all like to indulge a bit . . . what better way to make extra money than to cater to that universal craving for tasty food? Specialty food vendors, bakers, and gourmet fruit stands are solid ways for weekend entrepreneurs to cash in on this need, as are specialized services like custom cooking for professional people. Food trends emerge quickly. You can cash in on many of them as a weekend entrepreneur.

Long Shots—Great Ideas for Special People

Here are a dozen quirky ideas that won't just work for anyone, but maybe they will work for you! These ideas require special talents (like writing and publishing), special locations (gold mining country or tourist areas), or special skills. Real cash bonanzas if you have all of the special ingredients to make it work!

Moms at Home—Extra Money for Entrepreneurial Mothers

Many of the ideas covered in earlier chapters throughout the book are perfect for mothers at home with small children. In this section I detail the top ten ways for stay-at-home moms to earn extra income from home, and also select other great businesses that will fit this situation.

Thinking It Through

At the end of each chapter I have included a section called "Thinking It Through" in which I give a roundup of any special considerations that the businesses described in the chapter might require. Brass tacks elements like insurance, licensing, marketing, and any other hard facts are discussed. Read this section for important information before you make any decisions regarding which SAM will suit your needs, skills, and interests.

Each potential business is carefully explained in a simple fashion to help you decide if it is right for you. Any special requirements are explained, and any drawbacks revealed. In many cases I have included interviews with the real-life weekend entrepreneurs who have successfully used these ideas to add to their income. These folks give no-nonsense advice about just what it takes to make it work, as well as how much money you can expect to earn. Read about the success of country-crafter Darcy Tietjen in Anacortes, Washington; handyman Dan Newey in Sacramento, California; or even ten-year-old Dustin Smale! These successful weekend entrepreneurs also give lots of advice on marketing, finding customers, and getting paid. Start reading now and find the perfect SAM for you! Take a close look at the various chapters, flip to the section that seems right for your background, and find out how to join the growing ranks of the weekend entrepreneurs.

Chapter Two

Back to Basics— Elbow Grease and a Strong Back

Some of the best paying and easiest-to-establish SAMs for the budding weekend entrepreneur involve good, honest, hard physical work. Remember that group of people that we identified in Chapter 1 who just don't want to get dirty doing the basic things in life anymore? And the growing population of aging folks who are less able to do things for themselves? Well, those are definitely the target groups for clients and customers of many of the SAMs we will discuss in this chapter. So roll up your sleeves and get to work as a:

Car Detailer

Sunny Saturday afternoons used to be the traditional time for Dad and the kids to go out onto the driveway with a sloshing bucket of soapy water and a ragged towel rescued from the rag bin, armed with a coiled green hose, ready to give the family car its weekly washing. Well, times have changed. Mom and Dad are at the office and the kids are playing Nintendo™.

And although we all long for the way life used to be, we should also rejoice that yet another opportunity has been created for weekend entrepreneurs! Becoming a *personal car detailer* fills a real need in the marketplace for a number of reasons.

1. Many working people have less time nowadays to wash their cars themselves; they would much rather be out on the golf course or taking in a Saturday matinee.

2. With the uncertain economy, people are keeping their cars longer and postponing the purchase of a shiny new car. The car that they have been driving for years could use a good detailing to give it a new car look and help maintain its value.

3. People who own fancy cars love to lavish care and attention on them, but don't necessarily want to do it themselves.

4. Automatic car washes, although convenient and popular, just don't do the thorough job that a hand detailer can offer. It's like comparing a weekly quick-clean to a thorough spring cleaning!

5. Having a car detailed is a great way to improve its looks just before the owner puts it up for sale. That extra bit of shine helps keep the price up!

One of the very first weekend entrepreneurs that I ever met was my old college roommate, Margaret Cable. A full-time student, she supplemented her student loans by establishing several steady clients whose cars she would detail every other week. For a thorough car detailing, her rate was $50. I talked to Margaret about just what was involved in becoming a successful car detailer, and what exactly would be involved. Her advice was encouraging: "I made great money as a car detailer. After a few jobs I had a reputation as a super perfectionist, and that helped me get other clients. Starting the business was easy; I went to a high-end auto supply store and invested in their best car wash, car care, and wax products. Customers like to see you using top brands on their cars; it sure helps them write out that check for $50 at the end! Always use good chamois cloths on their cars; that looks impressive too."

Margaret's best customers were real estate agents. Agents frequently drive clients around in their cars and need to impress them with their shiny clean auto. For real estate agents who are women, Margaret's favorite finishing touch was a quick spritz of expensive perfume like Opium or Poison inside the car! That almost always brought a smile and a tip.

Tools of the Trade

To get started as a car detailer, here are the supplies you will need:

several spray bottles
towels for windows
toothbrush for detail work
instant brake dust remover
    spray
scrub brush with a long
    handle
portable vacuum cleaner
several chamois cloths
furniture polish for wood and
    plastic interiors
rubbing compound

window cleaner
squeegee
tire black
several good heavy-duty
    sponges
spray hose attachment
leather care products like mink
    oil
Ivory soap
wax
big box of Q-tips for the really
    fine detail work

You will have many of these things lying around your house now, but I will repeat the advice that the fancier the products you use and the better-looking your basic equipment, the higher the price the customer will be willing to pay. Think "image"!

Setting Rates

Personal car detailing service at the client's home or office should begin at $40, higher for trucks and vans. As you gain a reputation, or if you work in an expensive urban area, your rates may be somewhat higher. It is possible, but of course not required, that some of your customers may add a tip to the price when they pay you. And remember, this is a long way from the days when a kid would wash your car for a dollar. Act like a professional, do a good job, and you will succeed.

Finding Clients

Take a tip from Margaret Cable, try real estate agents first! Make up flyers and business cards advertising your personal car-detailing service and drop them off at real estate offices. Be sure to "chat up" the receptionist or office manager, perhaps you should even offer to do their car for free just to get the word around about your services. Do you live near a medical office complex? Put your flyers under the window of all those doctors' cars out there in the parking lot! Drop leaflets off at the doorstep in ritzy neighborhoods.

Satisfied customers are your best advertisement, and standing in someone's driveway doing a great job in full view of the neighborhood is like a free billboard and will help pull in the customers. Always behave as though someone were watching you (they probably are), don't play loud music, and don't let your friends hang around and talk to you while you are working. Work quietly and quickly, your customers will appreciate it.

Margaret Cable's Recommended Steps for Terrific Car Detailing

1. Wipe off all windows with a clean, dry cloth. Wash the interior windows and vacuum the interior.
2. Spray brake dust remover on the wheels.
3. Use the long-handled brush on the wheels, then rinse the wheels with a hose.
4. Wash the entire vehicle with mild soap like Ivory (but remember, the better the brand, the higher the price you can charge!), using sponges to clean the surface and a toothbrush to really clean the grill and the chrome pieces. Rinse the entire car.

5. Rub the entire car dry with a chamois cloth, wringing the chamois dry when necessary. Finish the drying process with ordinary terry cloth towels.

6. Wax the entire car (if a client requests that you use rubbing compound first, charge an extra $15). Modern silicon polishes are as effective as traditional wax, are easier to use, and have solvents to remove bugs. Use a good brand.

7. Wipe the entire interior with a damp cloth and use vinyl spray or leather treatment spray where appropriate. Lemon furniture polish is a good touch here. Empty ashtrays of trash and butts.

8. Do the exterior windows, using the squeegee to avoid streaks.

9. Apply chrome polish to the wheels to give them a brand-new look.

10. Apply tire black (carefully!) to all tires using a disposable sponge.

11. Wipe down exterior black plastic and rubber parts with furniture polish or mink oil. If you use mink oil, wipe down with a dry cloth afterward (otherwise dust will stick to the excess material).

12. Finished! Collect your pay and go on to the next car!

Personal car detailing is a terrific SAM that a dedicated weekend entrepreneur can start and succeed in with little or no money. It is also possible to go the high-end route by purchasing a franchise from a national company. Check the ads in many of the small business magazines and you will find the names of companies that offer franchises.

Christmas Light Installer

Once a year an opportunity to make excellent extra money appears—installing and removing decorative outdoor Christmas lights for folks who like the holiday look, but don't have the time to do it themselves, are too old to manage, or are afraid of heights. Full-time computer technology student Michael Ballard, 19, started Michael's Christmas Lights Services after several years of installing Christmas lights for family and friends. He decided that charging for the service would be an excellent way to earn extra money for college fees and books.

Setting Rates

Unlike costly decorating firms that provide the lights themselves as well as installation, Michael advises weekend entrepreneurs to work with their customer's own Christmas lights, "With the recession and everything, I think a lot of people just want to work with what they already have." Michael charges $20 for installation on a one-story house, and then returns several weeks later to remove them for an additional $10. A two-story house would run the owner about $50 for Michael's services. Extension cords are included in the price, but if clip fasteners are required he charges an extra $6.

Tools of the Trade

The tools required to run a seasonal business like this are minimal—a ladder, a staple gun, clips, and hooks. How much easier can it get?

Finding Clients

Start looking for customers in mid-November, perhaps even leafleting cars in grocery store parking lots while folks are doing their Thanksgiving Day shopping (check with the store's owner first). Picking out a fancy neighborhood in which to leaflet is also important. Many of these homeowners feel a real sense of competition with their neighbors when it comes to decorating for the holidays and they will be relieved to have professional help one-upping the Jones!

Tie-in Services

In addition to installing and removing lights, another handy service could be offered to your clients at the same time. For an extra $10 you could offer to haul away their Christmas tree and take it to a mulcher, thereby helping both the customer and the environment!

Cleaning Recreational Vehicles

RVs are everywhere! Retired couples vacation for weeks on end in their recreational vehicles, returning home happy but exhausted and only too pleased to pay someone skilled to give the RV a good post-trip cleaning. Specialize in cleaning only the interiors and build your reputation on that.

A thorough cleaning job in a medium-sized recreational vehicle will take approximately three hours. As you become more skilled and develop a routine you may be able to do a fine job in much less time.

Procedure

The preferred method of cleaning an RV after weeks on the road is as follows:

1. Always start with the dirtiest tasks—clean the freezer and refrigerator, stove and oven, and the entire kitchen area. Remove all items from kitchen drawers and cupboards and vacuum inside thoroughly before replacing.

2. Starting from the back of the RV and working your way to the front begin cleaning all of the surface areas like table tops, counter tops, the tops of shelves, seat covers, windowsills, and dashboards. Vacuum when necessary and then use a good vinyl cleaner and furniture polish on the proper surfaces. Check to see if the ashtrays have been used and empty if necessary.

3. Clean the entire bathroom thoroughly. This area really takes a beating during a long trip and the owners will appreciate a good job in this room.

4. Clean the entire sleeping area, vacuum carefully around the edges of the bed using crevice tools; dirt and sand end up here! Clean the closet area.

5. Clean all windows and miniblinds.

6. Moving from back to front again, do all of the floors with first the vacuum, then mop and wax.

7. Collect your pay from the satisfied owners, ask for recommendations of any other RVers who might also need your services, and head to the next job! And remember, smile everytime you see an RV out on the road. The owners will surely be needing your help soon.

Tools of the Trade

To clean the interior of an RV you will need the following supplies and equipment:

cannister-style vacuum cleaner with crevice tool attachments	sink scouring products
	oven cleaner
dust rags and cloths	vinyl cleaner
bathroom cleaner	window cleaner
floor cleaning products	empty garbage bags
mop	good sponge

Setting Rates

The price for a post-trip cleaning should be between $50 to $75 dollars. Large RVs and exceptionally dirty RVs should run closer to $80 for an interior cleaning. Washing the exterior of an RV is quite another matter and the price should be negotiated separately.

Finding Clients

Finding customers for this SAM is simple, just look up and down the street! RVs parked on the street and in driveways are simple targets for leaflets, either drop one on the front porch of the house or tuck it under the windshield wiper of the RV itself. Another great way to find clients for this specialized cleaning service is to head down to the local RV sales store. Once RVers have purchased their travel-home-on-wheels, they return again and again to the dealer to buy after-market gadgets for their RV. Posting flyers or business cards at the dealer is a terrific way to pick up business. Many of the dealerships have waiting room areas with bulletin boards sporting information about RV owners' clubs, groups, and get-togethers. This would be an ideal spot to post information about your RV cleaning service. Contacting the members of those clubs with flyers would also be a useful way to advertise your service.

Tie-in Services

In addition to cleaning the insides of RVs, it is also possible to specialize in detailing the outsides. I spoke to one entrepreneur who had been detailing RVs for several years: "You do have to specialize in RV detailing, because of the aluminum and so forth it is quite a bit different from detailing cars. It costs a lot of money to have an RV repainted, so what I do is 're-condition' it instead. A paint job for a motor home is going to run around $5,000, but I can totally recondition it for anywhere from $600 to $1,200." This fellow was very pleased with the extra income but was not at all willing to give me any details about his business. I guess it is so hot that he doesn't want anyone else doing it! So if detailing and reconditioning RVs sounds interesting to you, I'm afraid that you will have to go out and learn it all on your own.

Cobweb Cleaning and Removal Service

It's happened to everybody once or twice. You finally get up the nerve to invite the boss and his wife over to dinner, and after everyone has settled in to enjoy the evening you spy a cobweb hanging right over the sideboard on which your beautiful buffet dinner has been set. Those pesky cobwebs are

Procedure

Removing the cobwebs themselves is a straightforward process. First find them by looking EVERYWHERE! Ceiling corners, edges, window corners, and behind furniture are popular spider homes indoors. For outdoor spiders and their webs looking in eaves, window frames, door frames (every door frame in America has at least one spider web on it somewhere!), and light fixtures will give you a good start. You will soon develop a sixth sense about where to find webs, and you will learn the popular spots in your clients' houses. Spiders are brainless enough that they build webs over and over in the same spot.

Once you find a cobweb, you can't just shove the remover into it and scrub it free from the surface or you will end up with a bigger problem than before. Remember, cobwebs are sticky and dirt and dust cling to them, if you smear it into a wall you will now have to clean a sticky balled-up cobweb off of a wall. Instead, approach the cobweb delicately, as sportscasters like to say, with "touch." Use the remover to make contact with the cobweb, then slowly twist the remover while being careful to stay away from adjacent surfaces. The cobweb itself will stick to the remover; once detached from the wall you can slowly bring it away from the wall. Every so often you will have to clean the wound-up webs off your remover, this is what the paper bags are for! And what about the spider? Many times the spider will come off right down along with the web. Dispose of it in a reasonable way; smashing is not recommended!

To reduce your future workload you can use a pesticide solution. Discuss this in advance with your customer, though, not everyone feels the same about the use of insecticides. If you do use a bug killer use it sparingly; they are usually very strong and will leave an unpleasant odor.

Setting Rates

When setting rates for your cobweb removal service you must take into account the size of the house and the frequency of annoying, but they also present a SAM that can snare some extra cash for you! Why not run a part-time cobweb cleaning and removal service to make the world safe for casual entertaining? By offering your clients a biweekly or monthly cobweb service you will be tending to an unpleasant task that most people would happily prefer to hire out.

Cobwebs occur both indoors and outdoors; you can either specialize in one area or take care of the whole property indoors and outdoors for a larger fee. Style your cobweb service after the monthly pest spraying services, always arrive on the same prearranged day of the week or month, do the job, and leave behind a small payment envelope for your customer to mail back to you.

There is very little danger involved in removing cobwebs; the most dangerous element is that you may have to reach up into cathedral ceilings or outdoor eaves to track down those pesky spiders and their webs. In North America, the only spider that poses a serious threat is the black widow, which may be found in or near woodpiles close to the ground, often in a garage or similar area. Chances are that you will never see one of these small black and red-marked spiders, but do be careful regardless. Guard your personal safety with caution and the proper equipment.

Tools of the Trade

You will need the following tools for a cobweb removal service:

cobweb-removing tool	broom, bucket
extension pole	paper bags for your "catch"

Many home improvement, hardware, or even grocery stores sell a product called a "Webster" which has a big, soft circular brush about eight inches in diameter attached to a short extension handle. This handle can reach 8 to 10 feet off the ground, but you can add firepower to your tool by adding an extension pole to extend your effectiveness to 12 to 16 feet. Spiders and their webs can be pretty high off the ground!

the visits. Charge more for the first visit and then a smaller fee for recurring visits. Basic indoor service on a standard-sized house should be a monthly rate of $20. Two-storied houses, cathedral ceilings, or other quirks should add to the cost. Make sure you also consider the amount of time that the project will take you, be certain that your rates ensure that you make at least $20 an hour for your time.

Finding Clients

Spiders are everywhere, and so are your potential clients. Small neighborhood newspapers and newsletters are ideal for advertising a cobweb removal service. Distributing leaflets with information about your business to homeowners will also help get the message out.

Deck Cleaning and Refinishing

Anyone who has or has had a wooden outdoor deck knows how the weather takes its toll on it after a few years. "Weathering" may be desirable for some, turning the wood into an attractive neutral grey color, but most folks who have invested big sums of money into cedar or redwood decking prefer the handsome natural red color of the wood. Moreover, that "weathering" effect is caused by a growth of algae, making the deck very slippery when wet. This growth, along with dry-rot fungus, promotes decomposition of the wood in the same sort of process that causes wood to decompose naturally on the forest floor. For the average deck under normal conditions this weathering process begins to take its toll after about five years. It is so gradual that the homeowner might not notice it until his neighbor slips and falls coming up the walkway on a dark rainy night!

Ambitious weekend entrepreneurs can really "clean up" by starting a business cleaning and refinishing decks. To the delight of their satisfied clients, the homeowner ends up with safe and beautiful wooden decks that will last longer than those allowed to sit and rot.

Cleaning decks is hard work, but it is a safe, straightforward process with immediately recognizable results. In essence it is a hard scrub job with an oxidized chemical that kills and removes the algae growth and dirt down to the bare wood. You will need the following materials:

regular bucket	source of warm water nearby
stiff scrub brush	hose
sponge mop	high-quality rubber gloves
oxidizing deck cleaner	

The oxidizing deck cleaner can be obtained at most home improvement warehouses and at many lumberyards. There are two kinds—a white powder containing sodium peroxyhydrate sold in small jars and designed to be dissolved in warm water, and also a liquid form which contains oxalic acid and is sold in plastic bottles. The second type is also designed to be diluted in warm water before using. Both types work well, but the oxalic-acid type seems to work a little better and faster. A one-gallon bottle (enough to clean two good-sized decks) will cost around $10.

Procedure

Here is the best procedure for deck cleaning:

1. Hose down the entire deck.
2. Mix oxidizer cleaner into a full bucket of warm water. Mix only what you will need for an hour's work as the active ingredient weakens with time.
3. Apply to the deck with the sponge mop, about 150 square feet (15' × 10') at a time.
4. Allow to stand at least 15 minutes, but do not allow the surface to dry. If it is a hot day, hose the surface again to keep it wet until the time has elapsed.
5. Scrub with the scrub brush. If the compound has been allowed to sit long enough most of the algae will come

right off, as easily as scrubbing a dinner plate. Rub a little harder, and the original color of the wood will start to emerge. The amount of scrubbing required will vary with the age of the deck and the type of wood. On a really stubborn deck you might have to repeat steps 3 through 5.

6. Hose the cleaned section.

7. Repeat the process on another section of the deck. Soon you will develop a system of cleaning one section while allowing another to sit soaking for 15 minutes, thereby speeding up the job!

Setting Rates

How much should you charge for this terrific service? For an average size (20' × 30') deck you will spend four hours of hard work, plus your cleaning supplies and equipment; $80 is a fair price and a bargain to the homeowner. You have just extended the life of a major home investment!

Tie-in Services

The job—and the SAM opportunity—may not end with just cleaning the deck's surface. In addition to your basic cleaning service you can also offer additional services for more money. Dry-rot removal and protection underneath can also be done for an additional charge. And a good cleaning job won't last long unless a good deck stain or protective material is applied after cleaning. Therefore, you can offer your clients the following services:

1. Deck cleaning

2. Dry-rot removal

3. Protective sealing

4. Replace nails with longer-lasting screws

Dry-rot removal is a terrific service to perform, once again protecting their investment in their deck and ensuring that the deck itself will last for years. Add an extra $50 to your cleaning price for dry-rot removal. Dry rot usually appears on the underside of decks as a patch of white material. It often looks like old peeling white paint and is most commonly found where two pieces of wood join. Removing dry rot means scraping it off with a spatula, rasp, or similar tool. Once dry rot is removed, however, the clean area should also be sealed with a chemical preservative to prevent regrowth. There are many preservatives on the market; you should choose one that contains a fungus retardant. Copper naphthenate or other compounds that contain copper will work well and cost about $15 a gallon. Rubber gloves are a must with this procedure!

Most wooden decks are put together with nails, and therein lie two problems—nailed decks creak and shift and eventually nails will begin to stick up, with obviously painful results to the owner. Until the last few years the only solution was to go out with a hammer and pound those nails back down. Modern technology has now given us the cordless drill-driver, however, and replacing nails with deck screws can be a simple job. If you don't own a drill, you can rent one for the afternoon.

Remove the nails in the floorboards with a nail-removing crowbar and replace each one with a large deck screw. Deck screws cost $3 per pound, and you should charge your client 25¢ per replacement. Be aware, however, that it is sometimes difficult to remove nails without marring the deck surface. Discuss this with the owner beforehand in order to avoid a problem. It might be a good idea to draw up a disclaimer for clients to sign.

Finding Clients

To find clients for your deck cleaning and refinishing service you must target deck owners with flyers or circulars. Leafleting neighborhoods is one way, advertising in community newspapers is another, and many hardware stores have bulletin boards where you can let the local folks know about your skills.

Dog Doo Removal Service

Yes, this service does exactly what you think it does. What some people think is just a yucky and annoying job can mean scooping up dollars for you. Overlook the obvious jokes that your friends will make when they hear about your terrific new SAM and concentrate on making money. As our lives become more complicated, many of us turn to man's best friend for solace and comfort. After a tough day at the office, what could be better than curling up on the couch in front of the VCR with a dog sleeping on your lap? Unfortunately, although we enjoy having our pets around, we just don't seem to have the time to go out into the yard and pick up the . . . well, you know. And this is where you come in! As a dedicated weekend entrepreneur you can easily establish a Saturday or Sunday morning route of customers, dropping in just once a week to clear the yard of droppings.

Setting Rates

Average fees for this service can range from $6 to $10 per dog per week. Just think, if you have only ten steady clients with twelve dogs "producing" for you regularly, that adds as much as $480 to your bank account each month for just a few hours' work. Call this idea a SUPER SAM!

Waggin' Tails

I talked to Rhonda Jurkowski at Waggin' Tails about how she got started in the dog dropping removal business. "When I moved to California from Canada I had a few different ideas for businesses that I wanted to try, and this one seemed to have the biggest potential audience. At first I thought that my biggest group of clients would be handicapped people, but it turns out that by far the most typical client for Waggin' Tails is a double-income couple with kids. I guess they want the typical American family look with a couple of kids and a nice dog, but when it comes time to pick up after the dog they just don't have time."

Rhonda charges $6 for the first dog, and $3 for every additional dog in the household. Most clients have her come by once a week, but some like the yard cleaned two, three, and even five times a week! Six dollars five times a week—that's thirty dollars just from one customer alone! A business picking up dog droppings is perfect for a weekend entrepreneur, as most folks want their yard cleaned on the weekends.

Tools of the Trade

Not very many supplies are needed in this business, just a steady supply of medium-size garbage bags, gloves, a shovel, and a rake. How much simpler can life be? After two and a half years in business, Rhonda Jurkowski has her equipment down to a science—she uses a big lobby pan (the thing that you see employees at McDonald's using to sweep and pick up trash with at the same time) and a three-prong garden tool that she has lenghthened by adding a three-foot piece of PVC pipe. "Line the lobby pan with a garbage bag before you pick up a yard, and dispose of the droppings in the customer's own outdoor garbage can. If you take it away with you to dispose of somewhere else, you will need a permit for hauling hazardous waste!"

Finding Clients

The best way to find customers is to post notices in the window at your local pet stores and grocery stores. Ask the owner or manager for permission, of course. Letting veterinarians and dog trainers know about your service will also be a boost. The local dog pound is also a great place to advertise. Perhaps you could offer a one-week service free for a newly adopted dog; once the new owner gets used to your service it could become a steady account.

If there is no one else in your area offering the same service, the chances that you can get media coverage are very good. Call the newspaper and ask to speak to the business editor. He or she should be quite intrigued by your enterprising business and may very well write an article about it.

Another good bet for free media attention is morning radio disc jockeys. This is exactly the kind of thing that they would love to make jokes about on the air. Send a press release to their attention giving details about your service and be sure to include your phone number. They will, of course, make many silly jokes on the radio about you, but shrug it off and enjoy the free publicity.

Graffiti Removal Service

Graffiti on public and private buildings is an unfortunate fact of life nowadays, but the hardworking weekend entrepreneur can take advantage of this trend by cleaning up after graffiti artists! "You'll never have enough police to patrol graffiti," says Steve Lindner of Graffiti Control Services. "Most graffiti vandals want their mess to be seen. If you get rid of it, they might come back. But after a second time, they'll move on to another building."

Setting Rates

Depending on the size of the job, Lindner's fees can range from a low of $50 for a very small job to a whopping $10,000 for a full-scale graffiti-proofing treatment for a large building.

Procedure

To remove the graffiti Lindner uses several techniques, depending on the surface of the building:

1. On smooth surface buildings, the graffiti can sometimes be scrubbed off using basic cleaning solvents.
2. Brick surfaces need to be sandblasted with fine sand to remove the paint or ink.

3. Serious graffiti must be painted over. Match the original color by consulting with a local paint company for the best results.

Finding Clients

Chicago tuck-pointer Dan Webb works weekends as a graffiti remover. "This is a great business for part-time people. You can make $200 to $300 for an afternoon's work. My advice would be to keep it small and profitable." Dan also suggests that Merchants' associations and business associations like the Chamber of Commerce can be an excellent steady source of clients for a graffiti remover. Find out when the local organizations meet and attend meetings in order to meet members. Or you can just hop in your car and cruise the streets until you spot a graffiti-covered business; there are potential customers on every corner!

Steve Lindner has taken his part-time service one step further and developed a special coating for buildings that allows graffiti to be wiped off. He hopes to sell the mixture in large quantities to city maintenance departments across the country. But until Steve's coating protects every building in the land there will be plenty of opportunities for you to "clean up"!

Janitorial Service

"Janitorial work is a perfect small business for a weekend entrepreneur," George Bingham advises. "It is very easy to enter the market, and just as easy to get out when you no longer need the extra source of income. And the start-up costs are extremely low; to do most janitorial work in offices all you really need is a bucket, a mop, a vacuum cleaner, and some miscellaneous cleaning supplies. What could be easier?"

George started a small janitorial service several months ago as an additional source of income when the real estate business in California ran out of steam. "Get yourself a business card and walk out there and start knocking on doors in office buildings. Once you have signed up one client you can use that client as a reference to attract others." Running a small janitorial service at nights and on the weekends is a perfect way for a whole family to work together to make money. George says that it is becoming more and more common to see a husband, wife, and teenagers all cleaning together on the job. The work goes faster and everyone can contribute to the family business.

Setting Rates

Rates are very competitive in the janitorial business. Check to see what the average is in your part of the country before setting your prices. In the western states the standard rate is .5½¢ per square foot. Always insist on measuring the area yourself, George suggests. "In real estate everyone exaggerates the square footage when they try to sell an office building, but when hiring a janitorial service they always underestimate to try to shave costs! Be careful." The basic rate only covers vacuuming, dusting, and cleaning bathroom areas. More profitable aspects of the business are "tags," extras like carpet cleaning or window washing. These jobs are not done as a regular part of your nightly or weekly janitorial service, but rather once or twice a year for an agreed upon price.

Since the rates among janitorial services are so competitive, the best way to gain an edge on your competition is through superior service. Always be on time, do a thorough job, and leave the office looking undisturbed. This last piece of advice is crucial, as whenever anything is missing or broken in an office a finger will immediately be pointed at the janitorial service. Protect yourself by carrying insurance.

Tie-in Service

As with the housecleaning business, there are also emerging opportunities in the janitorial business for "green" cleaning methods that are easy on the planet. If there is not another environmentally correct janitorial service operating in your area this may be the way to distinguish yourself from the competition right away. Read the *Holistic Housecleaning* section in Chapter 6 in order to have a better understanding of this issue.

Educating Yourself

The ability to clean fast and well is important when you are trying to clean more than one office building a night. Best-selling author and cleaning entrepreneur Don Aslett has developed cleaning into a science, and many hints for fast methods may be found in his books.

> *Cleaning Up for a Living*
> Don Aslett
> Betterway Publications
> $12.95
>
> *Do I Dust or Vacuum First?*
> Don Aslett
> Writer's Digest Books
> $9.95

Organic Lawn Service

In Chapter 1, I talked about the need for a successful weekend entrepreneur to pay attention and spot trends and needs as they occur. The whole country is going "green" (another way to say "organic" or "environmentally sensitive") in the 90s, and businesses that cater to this need are truly on the cutting edge. And you don't get much more cutting edge than Christl Saed and her organic lawn service!

The Cutting Edge

After ten years in a dental office Christl decided to go back to school full-time and needed a part-time business to support her schooling. By combining her love of nature and the outdoors with her devotion to organic garden care, she has created a very successful business. "I'm not a 'mow and blow' operation, that is what my clients appreciate most," she said, as she described her business to me over coffee. "I use a hand mower to cut grass and a good old-fashioned rake to clean up the leaves. There are lots of people out there who are absolutely passionate in their hatred of gas-powered leaf blowers and the noise that they make. Exhaust, dust, and leaves blowing every-where, it is awful for the environment!"

By offering organic lawn care instead of the usual fare, Christl has found a profitable niche in an old-fashioned market. After just six months in the business, working just 20 hours a week, she is able to support herself while attending college. In addition to cutting lawns and cleaning up leaves, she also offers pruning and light trimming, weeding, removing annuals, and frequently makes suggestions to her clients about which plants might work best for them.

Two other services that she hopes to add once she gains more expertise are a composting and compost management ser-vice, and organic pest management. By expanding her range of services beyond cutting and raking she is able to make money throughout the winter season when grass grows slowly.

Tools of the Trade

Since this is by its very nature a "low-tech" business, start-up costs are low. In addition to a hand mower and several sturdy rakes, Christl has the following:

knee pads	pruning shears
spades and shovels	loppers
big plastic bags to move grass and clippings (but don't bag things permanently as it is terrible for the environment!)	hedge shears

Setting Rates

Rates are either hourly or a flat fee for regular customers. Depending on your area, you should be able to charge a minimum of $8 an hour for your service, and Christl suggests charging $10 an hour for one-time-only jobs.

Finding Clients

Advertising in publications that would appeal to the organically minded homeowner is your best bet for finding clients. Try small community newspapers or natural food co-op newsletters. Most food co-ops also have community bulletin boards where you can post information about your service.

"I love the fact that what I do is a part of the solution to the earth's problems," says Christl, "and I'm making more people aware of the environment at the same time. I set my own hours, work in the open air, and get paid to learn more about plants, soil, and moisture. As more and more people become aware of the connection between their lifestyle and the state of the earth, the opportunities for this kind of a service will increase dramatically."

Rain Gutter Cleaning and Maintenance

It is easy to overlook the significance of rain gutters—until they overflow, that is! Once the downspouts get plugged and leaves and water begin to collect inside, the chance that the gutter will tear off of the house increases dramatically. Working in the roofing trade gave Mike Ingram a chance to watch this process, and he soon realized that a second source of income was waiting in the gutter. "I learned first by cleaning out my own; that is the best way to learn. Hardware stores sell special scoops to clean rain gutters, and other than a big, tall ladder, that is pretty much all you need to do this! The bigger the ladder, the more money you can make. Reaching up to clean the gutters in tall Victorian homes requires a big, expensive ladder but it is worth it. I can easily make $150 a day doing this."

Mike's rates depend on the size of the house and the difficulty of the job, but he tries to charge enough so that he makes

$25 an hour for his time. Finding clients is not hard, he places small inexpensive ads in the local giveaway newspapers, "My first-ever ad got me three customers right away!"

Once customers contact you there is no need to try to give them a hard sell on your service; they know that they (and their rain gutters) need you. There is a two-step bidding process involved—Mike first gets a call from a potential client, drives out to size up the house and give the client an estimate, and then once the estimate is approved he returns on another day to do the work itself.

"You can definitely do this as a part-time extra business," Mike says, "but make sure that you get all of the appropriate licenses. Being bonded is a good idea, too. Gutter cleaners can also do minor repairs to rain gutters, but a contractor's license is required beyond a certain level. In the state of California, for instance, where Mike works, a noncontractor may only perform up to $300 worth of work on a gutter. Check with your state's contractors board to learn what rules apply to you.

Educating Yourself

For a solid tutorial in cleaning and maintaining rain gutters, check out the following book from the library or buy it in your local bookstore:

> *Reader's Digest New Complete Do-It-Yourself Manual*
> Reader's Digest Books
> $30

Tool Repair

In years past, traveling repairmen were a common sight. They combed the country knocking on doors and asking housewives if they had anything that needed fixing—pots and pans, odd pieces of furniture, or tools and equipment. Gone are the days of the tinker, but the need still exists for a skilled person to repair tools and sharpen saws! With the price of tools and other household equipment on the rise over the past decade, home-owners are protecting their investment by taking better care of their things. Every spring and fall there are garages full of lawnmowers, chippers and shredders, chain saws, weed trimmers, gas-powered leaf blowers, and all manner of garden and household tools that need a bit of mending. An enterprising weekend entrepreneur can easily line up grateful clients for a service that repairs and maintains tools by making convenient house calls.

Finding Clients

Customers may be found in your own neighborhood. Print flyers advertising your services as the local tool repairer and post them at nearby hardware stores, and leaflet the doorsteps of the area. When setting prices try to keep in mind that your house-call service is a convenience that should be included in the price, but do not overcharge for it. You want to make it easy for your clients to call you year after year whenever they get the yen to fire up that chain saw.

Tie-in Service

Once you have cleaned and serviced your client's tools you might offer an additional service—designing a shelving and storage system for their garage that will keep their tools neat and tidy all year round!

Educating Yourself

How does one learn to repair these things? It helps to have a good, solid understanding of the way that small engines work, but you can also learn from reading books and manuals. A basic introduction to the subject may be found in:

> *Care and Repair of Lawn & Garden Tools*
> Homer L. Davidson
> TAB Books
> $14.95

Tree Removal Service

Scott Standfill learned about how to handle trees while working for the U.S. Forest Service, and he has made good use of his tree skills since. A warehouse and shipping manager during the week, on the weekends he fires up his chain saw and goes to work as a highly paid tree remover. "I've been doing this for the past seven years, and it has helped bring in extra income for my family. On a good weekend I can make several hundred dollars for two days' work."

Scott gets most of his clients through referrals, but will sometimes stop and knock on the door of a house with a noticeably dead tree in the front yard. "They are usually happy to have someone offer to take the dead tree out, 'Oh, ya, I've been meaning to do something about that tree . . .' and my stopping and talking gets me the job!"

Setting Rates

Rates for tree removing vary according to the type of tree, the size, and the difficulty of the tree's location. Trees near power lines and houses are very difficult to remove properly and the customer pays accordingly. Scott's rates range from a low of $250 to a high of $500. His service also includes hauling the dead tree away, "I pass the charge at the city dump along to the customer," and for an extra fee will also include grinding the stump. He tries to plan the use of a rented stump grinder effectively—he will remove several trees one weekend, rent the grinder for one day the following weekend, and go back and grind all of the stumps in one day.

Tools of the Trade

To run a tree removal service, Scott recommends having the following equipment:

chainsaw	helmet and protective eyewear
pruning saw	heavy leather gloves and boots
ropes	

Tree-Removing Tips

Removing trees is a dangerous undertaking and you should not enter into this type of business lightly. A good way to gain experience working with trees is to take pruning classes from local nurseries and junior colleges. "Removing a tree is pretty much a heavy pruning job," Scott says, "but you just keep on cutting!" The chance that you might injure yourself while doing this or damage someone's property are also serious considerations. Landscape insurance is available to protect against this possibility. "Don't ever rush; always pay attention to the weather conditions. Wind is very dangerous, and so is a wet winter. And always keep your chain saw sharpened" are Scott's words of advice to fellow tree removers.

Weekend Handyperson, "Jack of all Trades"

Not every homeowner has the time or the skills or the inclination to fix the small things that need doing around a house, and when the weekend rolls around these homeowners are ready and willing to bring someone else in to fix what needs fixing. Can you pound a nail in straight, replace a broken window pane, or install a new lock? Sounds simple, but many of the talents and skills that you take for granted can be marketed to the thousands who need your help!

Dan Newey, a warehouse employee for Nissan, has been working as a weekend handyperson for the past five years. Install lights, fix plumbing, paint, put up shutters, you name it and Dan can do it. Dan can do it for $12 an hour, that is. Averaging 16 hours of his spare time a week, Dan works in order to make the payments on a rental home that he owns. So by working as a weekend entrepreneur, Dan is funding a great real estate investment that he could not otherwise afford.

Dan's description of what he does is typical of many weekend handypersons: "I really only have one or two major clients, but they all own rental homes so there is enough to keep me busy. If something needs fixing in their own homes

I get right to it, but pretty soon they remember a few other odd things that need fixing in one of the rental homes and it just goes on from there. I don't have any special training, most of what I know I learned from my dad. In order to succeed as a weekend handyman, you really need to be mechanically inclined. I found my steady clients by word of mouth, after five years I'm so busy that I have to turn away business sometimes. If I specialized in offering just one service like just fixing plumbing or just painting houses I know I could charge more, but I really enjoy what I do."

Tie-in Services

Among the services that a "weekend handyperson" could offer are the following:

>   small painting jobs both inside and out
>
>   simple repairs of lawn sprinkler systems
>
>   fence building, repair, and maintenance
>
>   basic locksmith work
>
>   annual removal and installation of screens and storm windows
>
>   install automatic garage door openers
>
>   caulking and weather sealing

To develop and sharpen your basic handyperson skills you should take courses in basic carpentry and plumbing. Doing work for free or helping while friends and relatives work on these kinds of jobs will also hone your skills to the point where you will feel confident charging someone for them.

Window Washer

When Mark Miyamoto and two other college friends couldn't find part-time summer jobs in Sacramento, they simply formed their own window-washing collective. "It was cheap to start up, I think that's why we chose window washing. We got started for around $30," Mark told me on the phone, taking a few minutes off from studying for his finals in agribusiness to tell me the details of having a window-washing business. "We bought a couple of supplies like squeegees, several spray water bottles, and a cobweb remover. We borrowed a retractable ladder, and mixed up our own secret window-washing formula. After testing the formula on our parents' windows to make sure that it worked we started to look for clients.

"Going door-to-door is not an effective method of finding customers, it takes too much of your time. Posting flyers at local grocery stores in our neighborhood was pretty effective, and an even more effective method was giving our flyers to local housecleaners to pass out to their clients. We got a lot of customers that way. Once we started working and the word got out that we did a good job, then we got lots of referrals. An extra $100 a week? Sure, we made that much and more!"

Setting Rates

Mark has quite a bit of advice for weekend entrepreneurs who are interested in starting up a part-time window-washing business: "The most difficult part in the beginning is deciding your price. It takes a fair amount of skill to appraise a job. Each house is different and the windows require different treatment. Those little paned windows are tough and take forever! Takes twice as long to wash that kind as the big picture windows. Two-story houses and houses with high ceilings are more, too. Our basic rate for an ordinary ranch-style house was $60. It would take between three and four hours to complete a house like that, inside and out. If we just did the outside, we would charge less. Spend some time checking out your competitors' prices. Our prices were comparable, and we promised our clients 'no streaks.' That was a tough promise to keep sometimes, but we did!"

Finding Clients

An interesting marketing technique that Mark and his partners used was a follow-up thank you note. Each and every one of their clients received a thank-you note in the mail a few days after the job was completed. Not only did this serve to reinforce the good work that had been done, it also encouraged their clients to recommend the window washers to their friends. And many did just that; the partners were busy all summer long. Their business was so successful that they plan on reviving it next summer too!

A part-time window-washing business works best during the spring and summer months. With the bright light streaming in, homeowners are keenly aware of just how dirty their windows have become and start to think of having them washed. The daylight hours are longer and part-timers can fit weekday window-washing jobs in. Saturdays and Sundays are ideal, of course, and it is possible to fit three or four jobs in during the weekend.

Alerting local realtors to your window-washing service is also a good move. As houses go on the market in the spring and summer months shiny clean windows help increase a house's "curb appeal."

Thinking It Through

All of the entrepreneurial businesses featured in this chapter have one thing in common—good, honest physical labor. Whether replacing deck screws, reaching for that high outside window under the eaves, or spending an afternoon soaping a fancy car, physical labor can be both financially and spiritually satisfying. Remember one other thing, though: you can also get hurt.

Liability Insurance

To protect both your own health and safety and to minimize the potential risk to your clients, it is advisable to carry special liability insurance. Many homeowners are wary of hiring unprotected, uninsured entrepreneurs and would never dream of allowing work on their house without proof of insurance. Should an accident occur, they have very real fears that they might be sued. Carrying your own coverage is one more selling point that you will have to offer. Ask your insurance agent about just what type of coverage would be best, and also seek out other weekend entrepreneurs to ask them about the insurance arrangements they recommend. This is a very important consideration and should be taken care of before you begin to do any work for others.

Bonding

In addition to insurance, you should investigate whether or not it would be wise to also be bonded. I spoke to several weekend entrepreneurs who felt that it was a genuine asset to be able to advertise the fact that they are bonded, and that it is an important element of their success.

The Local Hardware Store

Before you decide to launch one of the many businesses described in this chapter, I would suggest a trip down to your local hardware store. The neighborhood hardware stores, although they are rapidly disappearing, are great sources of information and research for hardworking weekend entrepreneurs. You will find bulletin boards posted with cards, flyers, and information. Check these to see if you will be offering a unique service or if there are already three or four folks in your area who do what you want to do.

Don't limit your research to the bulletin board; engage the employees in conversation and you will discover a gold mine of important information. "Thinking of offering a deck cleaning service, are ya'? Seems to me that there was a fellow around here used to do that but his wife got transferred and he moved away. He did all right, as I recall." Pay attention to the reaction of hardware store employees. If they don't think that a business idea will work in that area chances are they are right! Save yourself time and money and choose another business.

Introducing yourself to the local hardware guys will also help you with two other things—client referrals, and discounts on supplies and equipments. Once the employees are aware of your service and the quality of work that you offer they can be a rich source of business, sending clients your way month after month. And since they know that you are in business and will become a steady hardware store client yourself, you will be able to get trade discounts on the tools and supplies that you purchase.

Back-to-Basics Skills

To learn "back-to-basics" handyperson skills that you do not already know, or to brush up on the knowledge that you already posess, I recommend investing in the following book:

> Reader's Digest New Complete Do-It-Yourself Manual
> Reader's Digest Books, distributed by Random House
> $30

Using back-to-basics skills to make money will serve you well in the long run. These are useful skills that you can employ for profit when needed and just as easily put to rest when your need for extra income has passed. Basic skills and a willingness to work long and hard are a very rewarding combination.

Chapter Three

Old-Fashioned Money—Look to the Past for Your Financial Future

Why reinvent the wheel every time the tire needs changing? There are many great old-fashioned ways to make money in this world, everything from a community bake sale to the standard yard sale. There are also hundreds of services that used to exist and no longer do, goods and services that served a useful purpose but have been abandoned in our rush to embrace the new. Now is the time to reach back and dust off a few of those old ideas and turn them into twenty-first century sources of additional money!

Animal Sitter

With so many busy professionals taking off on business trips on a regular basis, who has time to take care of the dog? Pet sitting is an easy-to-start business that works well for a weekend entrepreneur. "Animal sitting is great for people who have flexible hours," suggests Heather Ireland, owner of Comfy Critters. "I get frequent calls for overnight visits; there are an awful lot of pet owners in this world who don't want their beloved doggy to have to stay alone at night while they are gone. Strange, but true."

Heather does warn potential dog sitters that you must have free time available both in the mornings and early evenings to take care of most animal-care tasks. An additional consideration is that you will be giving up much of your free time during the holidays, the busiest times of the year for animal-sitting services.

Setting Rates

Heather charges $25 for staying overnight in her clients' guest room, a great little SAM. Dog walking is another great extra source of cash; dog walkers charge $8 to $10 an hour and enjoy the extra benefit of getting exercise for themselves as well as for the dog.

Finding Clients

Clients can be found a number of ways: distributing flyers on neighborhood doorsteps; placing ads in local newspapers; leaving information at pet stores and veterinarians' offices; and don't forget the best advertisement of all, getting word-of-mouth recommendations from satisfied customers. It is important that you meet with the owners and their pets (particulary dogs) in the home before you take on sitter responsibilities. The owners will need to show you where the food is kept, where Sissy's favorite bowl is, and the hidden location of the toys and treats. Not all animals are well-trained or well-behaved, and caution is advised. "This is not a job for fearful people," says Heather. "You need to be extremely comfortable dealing with all kinds of animals; be cautious, but don't ever be fearful."

Animal-sitting services are catching on in popularity, so before you try to establish one in your area, you will need to scope out any possible competition. If there are too many animal sitters in one area or neighborhood, then none of them will be successful. Be very selective about the area; try to find one in which there is a high concentration of professional couples with purebred animals. A purr-fect SAM for animal lovers!

Antique and Collectibles Dealer

"It started years ago, when I was putting myself through beauty school," Donna Bates said, "I didn't want to go on welfare, so I started buying things at yard sales to resell at the flea market. I graduated to antiques and got interested in costume jewelry as a specialty. After I finished school and started my own shop I just couldn't get rid of the collectibles bug, so now I do it part time." Donna has a stall in an antique mall; she pays $105 a month for her portion and is required to work there once a month for four hours. It is a perfect setup for a weekend entrepreneur with an interest in antiques or period collectibles. The antique malls and galleries, now spreading coast to coast, are cooperative businesses in which all of the booth operators pitch in to work. The hours you are required to work vary according to your booth size; bigger booths may require as many as two days a month.

If you have a real love for antiques or enjoy spending your free time poking around yard sales and flea markets looking for special finds, then this is the SAM for you. Donna Bates' best find ever was a 14kt gold bracelet and ring for which she paid $2 each! Needless to say, she sold them in her stall for a great deal more.

Educating Yourself

Donna suggests starting by attending estate sales and yard sales to acquire merchandise, and also to acquaint yourself with the local antique market. How do you know what is a steal and how to price the bargains that you find? There are handy reference books that list prices on a wide variety of antique and collectible subjects to help you determine the retail value of the things you discover in your search. The best and most respected books are published by House of Collectibles.

Jewelry is very popular among collectors right now, both antique and collectible pieces from the 20s, 30s, and 40s. "Costume jewelry is much less expensive than the real thing," Donna explained, "and buyers know that old pieces are much better made than what you could buy in a department store now. I also think that people are attracted to the story behind the jewelry. When you buy a piece at Macy's you know that it came straight off of an assembly line somewhere, but when you buy an old piece you can let your imagination run wild about who it once belonged to and what their life was like. Royalty? An impoverished heiress who was forced to sell? You can make up all kinds of stories." In addition to jewelry, many collectors are attracted to fine pieces of china, and Donna observed that large pieces of furniture like dining room sets and bedroom sets seem to move the fastest.

Part-time antiques and collectibles booth dealers divide their free time between scouting for more merchandise and arranging things in their display cases. Once you have developed a reasonable inventory you can spend less time out scouting, but in the beginning it is important to spend both time and money combing your state for merchandise to resell. An established antiques and collectible dealer can have quite a steady little weekend business!

Beekeeping

Jerry Becker's father began keeping bees in 1919, and Jerry has been doing it himself for the past 30 years. As the assistant deputy state controller for the state of California, Jerry has a very important full-time job, but still finds the time to keep 250 hives busy and prospering on ranch and farm properties in northern California. Beekeeping can be very lucrative; the big money is in renting out hives of bees to orchard owners during the spring. "Thirty dollars per hive for three weeks, that's what the almond growers will pay," says Jerry. "With cherries and pears, the demand is not as high and the price for a three-week hive rental is only $10 per hive. I know a beekeeper up in Yuba City who keeps 17,000 hives; think about how much he makes during the almond pollination season. Around $510,000 for three weeks! Working with bees is very satisfying," says Jerry. "You are helping farmers and people raising natural foods, and meeting lots of interesting people. My son is quitting the computer business to go into beekeeping full time!"

Tie-in Services

In addition to renting his hives to orchards in order to help Mother Nature pollenate the trees, Jerry sells honey. "I move my hives around seven times a year. After the pollination season is over in northern California I send my hives down south to the orange groves. The bee's honey is then orange-blossom flavored, and that is what I sell to restaurants, cookie manufacturers, and bakeries in bulk. I probably sell about 32,000 pounds of honey a year in 30-pound bulk containers."

Other beekeepers sell their honey in one-pound jars at flea markets and farmers' market stands. Donald and Pat Hill of San Leandro, California, work several area farmers' markets throughout the year and sell jars of honey as well as handmade beeswax candles. Working just every other weekend, they add anywhere between $6,000 and $15,000 in extra cash to their budget every year!

Beekeepers can earn further profits by selling the beeswax directly to candle makers like me! (To learn more about beeswax candles, see Chapter 5, "Crafty Business.") Beeswax is used in a vast quantity of products, everything from ski wax to bullet flux. Royal jelly is another premium by-product of beekeeping, selling in natural food stores for premium prices.

Another skill that beekeepers can specialize in is swarm removal; ordinary folks call you to come and help when a swarm of bees invades their backyard. Removing swarms generally runs about $80, not bad for an afternoon's work!

Getting Started

Beekeeping sounds like a country-based pursuit, but it needn't be. Jerry Becker lives in the midst of a large California town and keeps his hives on farms nearby. "All you need is a cooperative rancher or farmer who has an out-of-the-way patch of land that you can use. I don't pay rent, every Christmas I give them jars of honey, honey candy, and candles."

Most large cities have beekeeping supply stores, just look in the Yellow Pages under "Beekeeping."

Educating Yourself

There are many solid books that will give you an introduction to the craft, among them:

Practical Beekeeping
Enoch Tompkins and Roger M. Griffith
Garden Way Publishing
$9.95

Honey: From Hive to Honeypot
Sue Style
Chronicle Books
$14.95

And there are nationwide magazines that serve beekeepers. These magazines are filled with articles and ads that educate and inform their readers about what is going on in the bee business. Mail-order supplies are advertised throughout, so if you don't live near a beekeeping supply store you can discover good sources in the pages of:

Gleanings in Bee Culture
The A. I. Root Company, Publishers
623 W. Liberty Street
Medina, Ohio 44256

Christmas Bazaars and Open House Craft Boutiques

"Although it always took place the first weekend in October, we would begin meeting with crafters and screening their work in January," Nancy Leneis explained. "My partner and I have always felt that the real key to our success was the high quality that we maintained. Nothing junky or tacky at our Christmas bazaar, that's what keeps our customers coming back every year for seven years!"

The Greenhaven Santa Boutique is an unusual annual bazaar. Crafters each pay $25 plus 10% of their proceeds to have their goods displayed. The organizers of the event do very well. "Yes," Nancy laughed, when I pressed her for specifics, "very well."

"This is a very rewarding and creative way to make money, one of the most rewarding things I've ever done. If you get 20 or 30 crafters together you can really have a big two-day show. The crafters always enjoy our show because they sell so much. One thing to remember is that inexpensive items always sell the best at these events. Make sure that you have a lot of things that are $5 and under. People will buy pricier things, of course, but the cheaper the item, the greater the sales!"

Greenhaven Tips for Successful Bazaar Organizers

1. Screen potential crafters' work, checking for quality and making sure that the final show does not have any imbalance (four dollmakers and seven tole painters, for instance).

2. Advertise the show extensively. Nancy and her partner kept a mailing list of shoppers from previous years and sent out personal invitations to these folks, inviting them to a special preview time. Ads in newspapers, flyers on telephone poles, and flyers left at other crafts shows help attract crowds.

3. Secure a good location and arrange for insurance. "We had our best location in a local school. The school had a bake sale table, and so since they were participating we were covered by their insurance policy instead of getting a special one-time rider on our own." Private homes and backyards can work, but gradually the more successful bazaars move to more professional locations.

4. Arrange the goods. "This was the real key to our success and the popularity of the boutique," Nancy explained. "We always had the crafters drop their goods off the night before, and then the show organizers would arrange everything in an appealing way. Instead of just individual crafters sitting behind tables showing off only their own wares, we had several theme rooms in which we built beautiful displays. A Christmas ornament room, a fall holiday room with stuffed pumpkins and turkey things for Thanksgiving and Halloween, a kitchen things room, a pink room, a blue room, and in each room the shoppers would just buy more and more!"

5. Handle the money. "People tend to buy a lot more when they are just writing one big check, and so early on we realized that there should only be one central cashier. As the event organizers, we would handle all of the money and keep track of who sold what. When all of the checks cleared we would total what each crafter had earned and send them one check, minus our 10% of course!"

The organizers are also responsible for securing a one-time resale license from the state. Since there is a centralized cashier, the individual crafters are spared the trouble of filling out the sales tax forms. Nancy pays the sales tax before figuring out the individual profits.

Model Home Craft Villages

Another variation on what Nancy and her partner do is to create a whole "craft village" in a housing development's model homes. One successful entrepreneur in northern California arranged just that, and made $60,000 in the course of one weekend! Here's how it works.

Approach the builders or developers of an upscale housing development that still has homes on the market. Tell them that you can bring thousands of people through their model homes in just one weekend. That ought to get their attention fast! Inside, the houses should be arranged in much the same fashion used by the Greenhaven Boutique. Instead of individual booths the rooms should be filled with artfully arranged merchandise, purchased from a central teller. If there are two or three model homes involved you can devote each one to a different theme.

Insurance should be less of a problem with this type of event. Talk to the developers about whether the attendees would be covered under their policy. And as for advertising, there is an awfully good chance that the developer will want to help you in a big way.

Everybody benefits—you get hoards of customers for the crafts, and the developers get lots of potential home buyers strolling through their model homes. Remember to take a percentage of your crafters' sales in addition to the participation fee, and you too might be on your way to big weekend bucks.

Custom Gardening

Growing up on a farm in California's Yolo county, Lisa Monckton developed an early love for the land. "My family has been farming the same farm for four generations, from my great-grandfather through to the present generation. On the farm we use modern agricultural techniques, lots of heavy equipment and chemicals, but over the years my own interests have turned to organic." After running a restaurant with her brother for many years, Lisa went on to become an agricultural inspector. As a hobby she started a large organic vegetable garden in her backyard to supply herself and her friends with tasty fresh produce. A year ago she founded a part-time custom gardening enterprise, Foodscapes. "The idea just came to me one day while I was fussing with a small onion plant. I thought of all of the people out there who would love to have produce growing outside their back door, but are too timid to get a garden started or don't have the time to establish one. There is a certain mystery to gardens that intimidates people. I realized that I could create a business that put gardens in for folks."

The Business of Foodscapes

Lisa grows seedlings at home and then transfers the medium-sized plants into her client's own garden. After first preparing the soil in order to encourage the plant's proper growth, she places the young plants together using the tightly spaced "French intensive method." A customer can go from a dry, weedy, overgrown garden one day to a beautifully planted vegetable or flower garden the next, an overnight transformation! When planting, Lisa follows what she calls the "five Ps" motto: Proper Preparation Prevents Poor Performance. A garden that has been installed by Lisa's methods requires little to succeed other than watering by the customer, delighting her satisfied customers year round with beautiful flowers, culinary and medicinal herbs, and organic produce.

On her initial visit with clients, Lisa quizzes them about the types of plants they would like to grow. "Tomatoes and garlic are by far the most popular requests," she says. But if a customer requests a plant that Lisa does not already have growing in her yard at home, she goes down to the local nursery and purchases it on a "landscaper's discount." Most work is done on the weekends, as many of her clients like to learn alongside Lisa as she works. Custom gardening is ideal for weekend entrepreneurs with a flair for growing. Lisa warns that it is hard and dirty work, but ultimately rewarding for garden lovers.

Tie-in Services

Lisa plans to add to her business services by teaching organic gardening workshops in the future. She also offers organic fertilizers as a sideline product.

Setting Rates

Lisa's rates for custom gardening are very reasonable—$3 per square foot includes the soil preparation, the small starter plants, and the actual planting. It is up to the customers to water and pick their produce! Although she feels that a price hike will be in order soon, she deliberately set her start-up prices low in order to attract as many first-time clients as possible. "I will have an easier time of it next year when I replant some of my customers' gardens. The soil won't need as much work as it did the first time and I can work much faster." Even though long-time customers require less care, Lisa's basic price remains the same.

Finding Clients

To attract clients she tried standard methods, flyers and advertising, with little or no success. "Publicity, that's the best way. I've had an article in the local newspaper and in the city magazine, and both have resulted in clients. As I grow the business I know that I will continue to build upon this base. Repeat business is a terrific money-maker for me. Organic gardening and organic produce are very hot right now, and I think that things will just continue to get better."

Cut Flowers for Sale

Lee Sturdivant lives on a modest 120' by 180' town lot on which she has successfully started a cut flower business to add to her income as a part-time ferry dock attendant. On a typical summer day she walks into her blooming garden and, sharp snippers in hand, cuts the following:

> 20 blue delphiniums, retail value $20
>
> 10 mixed bouquets, retail value $40
>
> 40 stems of sweet william, retail value $7
>
> 2 wedding bouquets, retail value $35

Over $100 in flowers from a garden that will be ready for cutting again the following afternoon!

Flowers are all around us in our lives, and weekend entrepreneurs with skill in the garden are well-placed to profit from Americans' love for decorating tables and sideboards with beautiful fresh flowers. Anyone with a medium-sized garden with good soil and reliable growing seasons can start and maintain a profitable SAM right outside their bedroom window!

Getting Started

To begin a cut flower business, you must first establish your garden. Among the most popular perennial flowers to grow for resale are yarrow, Peruvian lily, columbine, anemone, monkshood, daisy, spirea, bellflower, mum, larkspur, carnation, foxtail lily, baby's breath, lavender, lupine, peony, oriental poppy, phlox, freesia, lobelia, orchid, ranunculus, spiderwort, dahlia, and evening primrose varieties.

Perennials usually produce only greenery the first year, not flowering until the second year. Growing annuals in your flower garden as well will allow for a much faster production time. Both annuals and perennials should be started from seeds as the most inexpensive way to begin your for-profit gardening. Popular annuals include hollyhocks, snapdragons, bachelor's buttons, sweet williams, foxgloves, cosmos, statice, stocks, marigolds, and zinnias.

Finding Clients

Once your garden is overflowing with mature blossoms you are ready to find customers. Small markets can be approached about carrying your ready-made bouquets. Offer to service the in-store display frequently to keep the flowers looking fresh and remove any drooping unsold bouquets. Farmers' markets are also terrific places to sell bouquets; after all, you are a farmer of sorts! Become familiar with the florists in your area; they might also be interested in unusual old-fashioned garden flowers to supplement their greenhouse-produced roses. If you live in a well-situated part of town and your garden is visible from the street you might also begin to attract private customers who will come to you for fresh flowers for special occasions. Large-scale flower gardens in the country have even been turned into successful "U-Pick-It" operations by their owners!

Educating Yourself

Lee Sturdivant was so pleased by her success as a cut flower grower that she sat down and wrote a very detailed book in order to encourage others to try this business. I highly recommend her book to anyone with a green thumb and an interest in greenbacks!

> *Flowers for Sale: Growing and Marketing Cut Flowers*
> Lee Sturdivant
> San Juan Naturals
> P.O. Box 642
> Friday Harbor, Washington 98250
> $10.95

Foraging the Wild for Profit

Like our pioneer ancestors before us, it is still possible to forage in the wild. But, instead of foraging for wood to keep us warm and berries to keep us fed, we can forage for profit! No matter where you live, there are things growing near your neighborhood that can be picked for free and sold for a terrific profit, or else used as an element in a craft project that you can sell for a wonderful SAM. And foraging is not just for women—the *Wall Street Journal* recently featured Oregon lumberjacks who forage pinecones to add to their bottom line. Most small pinecones sell for 25¢, but some large pinecones sell for as much as $12 in Japan.

A Sixty-Dollar Walk in the Woods

On a recent trip from California up through Oregon and Washington my head was constantly turned by the sight of wildflowers, beautiful autumn leaves, flowering sagebrush, pinecones, and evergreens lining the backroads just waiting to be harvested by an enterprising weekend entrepreneur. A half-hour hike in the woods with my husband yielded an abundance of small hemlock cones and a good supply of lichen (or goat's beard). Two hours' worth of work with a needle and thread and a $4 grape vine wreath form combined with my foraged materials to produce a beautiful "Pacific Northwest Christmas" wreath, which I sold a few weeks later at a craft fair for $30. A few minutes of picking bunches of wild strawflowers from the side of the road on a mountainside near Ashland, Oregon, also brought a tidy profit when I bound individual bunches with ribbon and sold them at my candle booth for $1 per bunch. At the same craft fair I also sold small bunches of heavenly scented eucalyptus leaves (which I found hanging from a tree in my own backyard) for $2 per bunch. The only extra touch I added to my foraged greens and flowers were small satin ribbons to bind the ends and give them a more finished look. I added an extra $60 of pure profit that day, just by taking a walk in the woods. Thank you, Mother Nature!

What to Look For

Among the things that can be foraged in the wild for your financial benefit are

acorns	pine cones
mistletoe	thistles and teazels
moss and lichen	fallen wood
wild mushrooms	dried grasses
berries	pussy willows
wildflowers	wild roses
autumn leaves	heather
evergreen branches and boughs	holly
eucalyptus	manzanita

rocks and pebbles	pine needles
seedpods	owl pellets
cattails	mugwort
wheat	

Many of the things that you pick up on hikes and walks in nature can be used in handcrafted projects like wreathes, woven baskets, swags, and decorative hangings. Christmas is an especially good time to forage to your advantage. To learn more about how to craft wreathes and dried floral arrangements from foraged materials, I recommend several books at the end of this section.

Finding Clients

Christmas gift boutiques, tree lots, and crafts fairs abound and are the perfect place to sell your wares. If you really dedicate yourself to developing a reputation for quality work and original creations, then the catalog market is also worth trying. Flipping through a selection of high-quality national mail-order catalogs filled with holiday merchandise, I saw countless products that were made from materials that could have been foraged for free from a nearby forest, field, or meadow. Among the high-ticket items included that an enterprising weekend entrepreneur could make from free materials were:

eucalyptus wreath (eucalyptus leaves layered in a fish-scale pattern and secured by bronze boat nails) $46

alpine wreath (made from white larkspur, California lace moss, salal and melaleuca leaves, sarracenia lilies, sage, and pinecones woven on a base of huckleberry vine) $69

pinecone tree (clusters of pinecones joined to form a rustic tree) $18

winter woodland wreath (cedar, oak leaves, salal, sweet annie, ferns, and boxwood accented with hazelnuts, lotus pods, and large white roses) $56

summer spray (field-dried grasses, sunflowers, roses, bay and melaleuca leaves, blue larkspur, bound with raffia) $52 fresh holly wreath (freshly picked Oregon holly leaves and berries) $36

harvest garland (oak leaves, bay, pepperberries, pepper-grass, and marjoram tied with raffia) $46

mistletoe and eucalyptus kissing ball $23

two-pound bag of scented pine cones $13.50

pinecone door hanger $16

pinecone wreath (traditional wreath made from pinecones ornamented with kitchen spices—orange peel, cinnamon, assorted nuts, and star anise) $69

fragrant pomander balls $4.95

fall colors wreath (oak leaves, eucalyptus, bay laurel, white California moss, seedpods, bittersweet) $59

preserved autumn leaves $9.95

And the best foraged item of all in one of the catalogs? Rocks that had been painted to look like cats: "Watershaped through the ages, gathered from Appalachian creeks, hand-painted, signed, and dated by the artist. Terrific gift for people who love cats, rocks, or pets, or anyone who uses paperweights! Each pet is about five inches long, weighs up to one pound and no two are alike." These painted rocks sold for $17.50 each. I hope you are starting to get the idea that there is a lot that can be done with what nature provides!

Another steady source of customers for your foraging dis-coveries are florists. Gardening is the "sport of the nineties," and high-end gardening stores are opening up all over. These stores would also be potential customers for well-crafted items made from foraged materials.

Tie-in Services

The *Wall Street Journal*, which ran the front-page story about foraging loggers, also featured a lengthy story on foraging for owl pellets (owl regurgitations), sought for use in high school biology classes. It is no longer politically correct to dissect little frogs, and owl pellets are chock full of tiny mouse bones and snake skins guaranteed to intrigue budding scientists. Scientific supply houses pay top dollar for owl pellets, and successful pellet foragers are very secretive regarding old dusty barns they are finding fortunes in.

Respecting the Wild

When foraging in the wild, there are a few rules that you should keep in mind. The first, and most important, is to research your finds. Always know what you have collected and whether or not it is safe. Wild mushrooms in particular are very dangerous things and should never be collected and sold unless you have familiarized yourself with all of the varieties. Mushrooming courses are sometimes available in areas where wild mushrooms grow, and there are numerous local mushroom-collecting societies that you can join to learn more about it. If you establish yourself as a wild mushroom forager with a good reputation for safe mushrooms you can develop a devoted clientele among gourmet restaurants.

The other rule to keep in mind is that, despite the fact that so much of what grows in nature seems like it should be available for us to take, it is not. Before collecting wild flowers, grasses, or anything else from the side of a highway, check with the highway patrol to see if this concerns them. Be sensitive to private property and respect the rights of others. Do not attempt to forage on land that you suspect may be privately owned without first checking with the owner. And remember that it is illegal to remove anything from a national park or forest. Keep these rules in mind.

Stern warnings aside, I encourage you to start to look at the world around you in a whole new way. Once you start to see the potential products or materials waiting for an enthusiastic weekend entrepreneur (and helpful family members!) to scoop them up, you will be astonished at what nature provides us. Get busy!

Educating Yourself

Here are useful books about foraging and crafting from foraged materials:

Taming the Wild Mushroom: A Culinary Guide to Foraging
Arleen and Alan Bessette
University of Texas Press
$24.95

All That the Rain Promises, and More . . .
A Hip Pocket Guide to Western Mushrooms
David Arora
Ten Speed Press
$15.95

Herbal Wreathes: More Than 60 Fragrant, Colorful Wreathes to Make and Enjoy
Carol Taylor
Sterling/Lark
$12.95

The Complete Book of Nature Crafts:
How to Make Wreathes, Dried Flower Arrangements, Potpourris, Dolls, Baskets, Gifts, Decorative Accessories for the Home, and Much More
Eric Carlson, Dawn Cusick, and Carol Taylor
Rodale Press
$24.95

Year-Round Wreathes: Creative Ideas for Every Season
Richard Kollath
Facts-on-File
$21.95

Baskets from Nature's Bounty
Elizabeth Jensen
Interweave Press
$24.95

Garage Sales and Yard Sales

For weeks I'd been carefully saving up money for an autumn trip to the Pacific Northwest. I was pleased with the size of my savings account and congratulated myself on a job well done—until my car suddenly needed several hundred dollars of emergency repairs! Overnight the vacation money that I'd squirreled away was gone. Rather than cancel a trip I was looking forward to I decided that an emergency SAM was needed—a garage sale!

Nothing can beat a yard sale or garage sale for instant cash. Look around your house, poke around in the garage, peer into the back of your closet, and I am certain that you will discover many things you once needed but haven't used in years. "Gee, do I really need my scuba weight belt? I haven't been diving since 1990! And these bags of cassette tapes, when did I last listen to 'Men at Work'?" I was ruthless in my appraisal of what should stay and what should go, and after only two hours work I had collected quite an impressive array of goods.

Keys to Success

Newspaper advertising always pays off for a yard sale. Your best customers will be early birds (who we now know are in fact weekend entrepreneurs out scouting for super deals on things that they can resell at their flea market booth or refurbish and sell at an antique mall) who arrive close to dawn to peer at your goods. Throughout the day you will notice carloads of people consulting the classified ads. The $20 or so that you spend on a garage sale ad brings in much greater customer traffic.

To make your sale look larger and therefore more visually enticing to passersby, invite your friends to bring their extra things over to sell. Just about everyone has a few things sitting around that they no longer need, and they would be happy to let you sell them for a small percentage. When they stop by to deliver their things, don't be too surprised if they buy something of yours before they leave!

The evening before your sale is a great time to sort through things and price all of the items. This should all be done beforehand; once your sale gets going you will not have time to pay attention to these small details. Decide which priced items you will remain firm on, and which items you will be willing to bargain on in order to get them out of your garage for good! Make sure that you have at least $20 in small bills on hand for tomorrow's sale, and a few dollars' worth of change.

Sale Day

The morning of your sale you will get up very, very early. This is a key element to yard sale success; posters and signs must be posted around the neighborhood before 8 a.m. in order to really draw. Make sure that your signs clearly point the way to your house, and that they are readable from a distance. During the course of the day it is a good idea to send a friend or spouse around to check on your signs and make sure that they are still posted.

The actual sale will go by very quickly. Time seems to fly as more and more people mingle around on your front lawn asking about prices, checking over bargains, and then handing you crisp green dollars. Few things are as satisfying as the ever-growing wad of dollar bills in your jeans pocket on the day of a garage sale. At the end of the day I drag the leftovers back into the garage to await the next sale, and I carefully remove my signs from the neighborhood telephone poles. Then it's time to rest and count my money!

Steps to a Successful Yard or Garage Sale

Beforehand:

1. Choose your date and place your ads.
2. Select items and begin pricing.
3. Make large signs for the neighborhood.
4. Get quarters, dimes, and nickels, and single bills for change.

The day of the sale:

1. Get up very early and put signs out.
2. Haul stuff onto the front lawn or driveway.
3. Enjoy the action!

A great resource book on successful garage sales is:

The Garage Sale Book
Jeff Groberman and Colin Yardley
Prima Publishing
(916) 786-0449

Herb Farming

America is wild about fresh herbs, and small-time herb farming is an ideal business for a weekend entrepreneur. Using just your own backyard (or in some cases your own basement or garage) it is possible to grow enough herbs to generate a SAM that produces an extra $50 to $250 a week. Gives a whole new slant to the expression "growing a business"!

There are many culinary herb varieties, but not all are popular with cooks. The best herbs to grow now are basil, dill, French tarragon, mint, oregano, rosemary, chives, parsley, and thyme.

One unusual plant with spectacular financial possibilities is ginseng, a medicinal herb. Long sought after in Asia, cultivated ginseng is now also grown in some parts of the United States. The price per pound varies from year to year and depends on the quality and type of ginseng root, but can be anywhere from $30 to $150. That's right, $150 per pound. Ginseng is a long-term investment though, it takes up to eight to ten years before your first crop comes in. Last year the total cultivated ginseng export from the United States was 1,289,000 pounds, valued at $62 million. With the growing interest in alternative medicine and healing both in America and abroad this is a market that is certain to expand.

Finding Clients

There are plenty of ways to make money with the herbs that
you grow.

1. Sell them wholesale to small local grocery stores and
   specialty food markets who would like to offer a good
   selection of fine organic, locally grown herbs to their
   customers. As more mainstream cooks begin to use
   herbs even grocery stores that traditionally stocked
   only parsley are beginning to branch out into basil, dill,
   and cilantro.

2. Sell directly to the customer at retail prices at farmers'
   markets and roadside stands. In addition to selling cut
   herbs for cooking you might also offer small potted
   herb plants. Dried herb packets, potpourris, herbal
   vinegars, sachets, and mixed herb and flower bouquets
   are just a few of the other products that you could also
   sell at your stall.

3. Restaurants that specialize in gourmet dishes are also
   a ready market for your locally grown herbs. Approach
   the chef and offer a steady supply of high-quality "just
   picked" herbs and you will make a friend for life. Bakers are also adding herbs to breads and rolls and are
   potential wholesale customers.

4. Herbalists and aromatherapists are emerging everywhere. Fresh herbs are a critical part of what they offer.
   Acquaint yourself with the field and find out which
   herbs would be of most use to them.

5. Caterers can also be a steady source of clients. Catering
   is a very competitive business and canny caterers are
   always looking for ways to distinguish themselves
   from their competition. Why not convince a few of
   them that they can have the freshest herbs around?

6. Herbs are sometimes used in teas, most notably
   chamomile. Offering dried chamomile tea either for
   drinking or as a hair rinse would be an ideal side product to fresh culinary herbs.

7. Mail-order sales of potted plants and unusual seeds can
   also be a potential source of revenue once you have a

well-established herb garden. This would require a space larger than the average backyard, however.

8. Herbal cosmetics are gaining in popularity once again (in times past they were the only kind available!). You can research and develop your own herbal cosmetic products to sell retail or contact herbal cosmetics companies about wholesale sales of your fresh herbs.

While researching this chapter I became entranced with herbs and the vast number of products that can be developed from your own crop. Catnip toys, even! Grow catnip and sew it inside of cute fabric toys that you can either sell yourself as a sideline or offer to local pet stores on a wholesale basis. The fresher the catnip the more the cat loves it, so the pet stores would actually be offering their customers a superior product. Try it and tell me how it goes!

San Juan Naturals

As you can see, herbs have unlimited potential as a cash crop and are easy to get started right away. I spoke to Lee Sturdivant of San Juan Naturals in Friday Harbor, Washington, about how she got started as an herb grower: "I started growing herbs for my own kitchen, and began giving the overflow away to friends. It was a short step from supplying friends for free to supplying local restaurants for profit! Like lettuce, fresher is better when it comes to herbs. Local restaurants and grocery stores prefer buying from local growers because, not only is it very fresh, but they don't have to pay shipping costs. Growing herbs is definitely a great way to be a weekend entrepreneur; because of the growing cycle you don't have to commit yourself to a year-round business."

Sun Moon Botanicals

Herb farmers have a built-in audience, and many of the businesses that have a need for herbs like restaurants, bakers, and herbalists really do prefer dealing with a local producer. Danuta

Lake, an herbalist in Anacortes, Washington, told me that she really likes buying herbs from local growers for her business Sun Moon Botanicals. "I like knowing where the herbs come from and the conditions under which they were grown. I also like to support other local people." She recommends that small-time herb growers stick to the basic European herb varieties since that is the greatest need. So don't be afraid or intimidated about approaching these folks for their business; they will be pleased.

Educating Yourself

Growing herbs is not difficult, and there are several good books available to help you develop your skills. Look in your local bookstore or library for the following titles:

Herbal Bounty
Steven Foster
P.O. Box 32
Berryville, Arkansas 72616

In addition to books about growing herbs, several books are now available to help you with the business of selling herbs.

Pay Dirt: How to Raise and Sell Herbs and Produce for Serious Cash
Mimi Luebbermann
Prima Publishing
$12.95

Profits from Your Backyard Herb Garden
Lee Sturdivant
San Juan Naturals
Box 642
Friday Harbor, Washington 98250
$10.95

Backyard Cash Crops: The Sourcebook for Growing and Marketing Specialty Plants
Craig Wallin
Homestead Design, Inc.

P.O. Box 1058
Bellingham, Washington 98227
$14.95

If you live in an area that does not have a well-stocked library or bookstore, Ag-Access in Davis, California, has a catalog featuring a variety of agricultural titles for growers. Call (916) 756-7177 for a copy of their catalog.

As more people take up herb farming as a business or a hobby, more publications devoted to herbs seem to appear. The best magazine is *The Herb Companion,* filled with articles of interest to herb growers and herb fanciers including lots of information and advertising from a variety of seed and plant sources. In addition to magazines sold on newsstands, there are several newsletters available that cater to the business of herb growing. These newsletters are filled with valuable information on marketing and selling herbs:

Specialty Crop Digest
Homestead Design, Inc.
P.O. Box 1058
Bellingham, Washington 98227

The Business of Herbs
Northwind Farm
Rt.2 Box 246G
Shevlin, Minnesota 56676

The Herb Growing and Marketing Network
publishers of both *The Herbal Connection* and
The Herbal Green Pages
for information call (717) 898-3017

To learn more about ginseng and whether it can be grown in your area, you can write for information to either of these sources:

Buckhorn Ginseng
Rt. 4, Box 336
Richland Center, Wisconsin 53581

Hsu's Ginseng Enterprises
P.O. Box 509
Wausau, Wisconsin 54402

Pet Food Delivery Service

As the pace of life speeds up, there are so many promises that go unkept—like the vow you took to feed your animals only that nutritionally sound pet food that requires a special trip to the vet's office to buy. Sometimes you remember, but all too often Fido and Sissy eat whatever you managed to pluck off the shelf at the neighborhood grocery. But what if someone would bring that fancy pet food right to your door whenever you needed it? What a great idea!

Pet Meals on Wheels

Pet Meals on Wheels, owned by Kristine Backus, provides exactly this service. While also working part time as the head of the computer lab in an elementary school, she spends several hours a week driving her pickup truck filled with Science Diet, IAMS, Nutro, and other superior pet food brands to service her 250 regular customers. She delivers a minimum of 20 pounds of food at a time. Instead of charging a delivery fee, she merely marks up the price of the food. Her dog Kitzy accompanies her on her route, adding to the laid-back and "stress-free" nature of her business.

Finding Clients

Most of Kristine's customers are affluent people who are short on time but long on ideas about how their lives should be, only the best for these folks and their pets. Word-of-mouth, flyers dropped on doorsteps or given out in veterinarians' offices (only offices that don't already sell food!), and networking with local pet sitters and dog groomers have brought clients her way. "Find a neighborhood filled with lots of houses and blanket the area with flyers. I go out and do it on my roller skates!" Kristine says. "That way you can pick up several clients in the same neighborhood and have a more efficient route."

Educating Yourself

Delivering pet food is a business for animal lovers and people who genuinely care about animals' health and happiness. You will need to educate yourself on the upscale brands available and the relative advantages of each brand. It is also important to educate yourself about the competition, how much do the local pet food stores charge for the brands that you will be offering? Find pet food wholesalers in your area by looking in the business-to-business phone directories, and keep in mind that some retail stores might also be willing to sell to you at wholesale if your orders are large enough.

Kristine Backus has written a start-up manual for those who would like to get into a business like this. It is available for $47 postpaid from:

Pet Meals on Wheels
P.O. Box 1526W
Rocklin, California 95677

Real Estate Agent's Helper

Real estate agents can't be everywhere at once, no matter how hard they try. Holding open houses, showing property, meeting with lenders, and prospecting for new clients is a non stop job. To do a more efficient job it is common for real estate agents to hire freelance assistants to help them with some of the less technical parts of their work.

"Open House" signs sprout like mushrooms on the weekends and every one of those signs symbolizes a potential opportunity for a SAM. "I hire an assistant to help me with an open house on an average of once a month," says Margaret Greenberg, "whenever I have more than one home that I am trying to market. I work one open house, and the assistant works the other. The job is very simple—just greet folks as they enter and hand them a brochure about the house. Because the assistant is not a licensed real estate agent he or she *cannot* answer questions, but rather spends the entire afternoon saying, 'I can have the listing agent call you to answer that question.' It's a pretty simple way to make money on a weekend." Margaret pays her assistants $30 for three hours' work. Another northern California realtor, C. Nikki Reuppel, also hires assistants when needed. She requires her assistants to first stop by her office and pick up the "open house" signs, place them on the street according to her instructions, hold the "open house," and then gather and return the signs at the end of the afternoon. "I can double my effectiveness," Nikki claims.

Finding Clients

Sure sounds easy, but how can one find work as a freelance real estate agent's helper? Start with any real estate agents that you might know. Suggest to them that their time is more profitably spent on activities other than holding homes open on weekend afternoons. As Margaret Greenberg sums it up, "An agent's time is most profitably spent prospecting. Open houses are too slow. It is just not efficient. I could be making contact with 50 potential prospects on the phone in an afternoon instead of standing in an open house meeting 5." Remind agents that you can help increase their efficiency and effectiveness. If you do not know any real estate agents personally, then make it a point to stop in and meet them when they are holding open houses! There they are, just waiting for you to offer to help.

Tie-in Services

In addition to holding open houses there are a number of other nonprofessional tasks that you can offer to perform for real estate agents: dropping off brochures and flyers, helping with holiday promotions (many agents like to distribute flags on the Fourth of July), and if you have computer skills, helping with newsletters. Telemarketing (cold calling to find prospects for the agent) for real estate agents is another possibility. All of these tasks can easily be done during your available hours.

Tips for Success

Important things to remember about working as a real estate agent's assistant:

1. **Appearance.** You must be neat, clean, and professionally dressed—a suit and tie for men and a business suit or dress for women.

2. **Speech.** You must be well-spoken and able to communicate easily with strangers.

3. **Manners.** You must be well-mannered and polite at all times.

4. **Promptness and reliability.** You must be on time; if an agent needs you at noon, be there!

5. **Professionalism.** Remember that you are not a licensed real estate agent and cannot talk about price or terms. Do not attempt to answer technical questions or you and your agent will be on dangerous legal ground. Please check into the restrictions and regulations that apply in your state.

Thinking It Through

Many of the ideas in this section are no-brainers, simple one-shot ideas like yard sales, but others are much more complicated and time-consuming. Before embarking on a business like custom gardening or beekeeping, think long and hard about your own lifestyle and your commitment to creating a successful SAM.

Time is important to all of us, and we value the free time spent planted on the couch with the remote control in one hand and a big bag of popcorn in the other. Some of these old-fashioned ideas would require large investments of time to achieve success, so please be realistic about how much of your time you are willing to devote. There is no sense in spending money on beehives or planting an herb patch in the backyard if ultimately you decide that it is too time-consuming to pursue. Sit down and do an honest evaluation of how much time you will be willing to spend and make sure that you choose a SAM that fits that mold.

Also examine your immediate cash needs. Can you afford to wait until a crop grows to maturity or bees produce their honey? If your landlord is banging on your door for the rent or you have to pay for your son's braces now, a yard sale is a better SAM than gourmet vinegars. Once you have taken care of the immediate cash crunch, perhaps then you can turn your attentions to an entrepreneurial enterprise with a more long-term payout.

Remember, there are many more old-fashioned ways to make extra money than the ideas that I have presented here. Think back to your own childhood, or stories that your parents and grandparents have told about the way "life used to be." Can you think of a successful business that seems to have disappeared over the years for no apparent reason? Let history be your guide, and you may well discover an old-time gold mine!

Chapter Four

Teen Stuff—Cool Ways to Earn Cool Cash

Why let your kids sit around and envy their friends for the cool stuff that they have when you can encourage them to get out of the house and earn some extra spending money of their own. Adults love to be approached by enterprising kids, and if the idea is unique, the media loves it too. This chapter lists many ideal projects and entrepreneurial undertakings that are perfect for teenagers (and sometimes even younger kids) with enthusiasm and drive. So tell your kids to quit bugging you about a bigger allowance; loan them this book and tell them to get out there and start a business.

Annual Pumpkin Patch

I noticed it driving home from the office late one afternoon, a series of hand-lettered signs attached around a fence advertising "Dusty's Pumpkin Patch," with hours for the following Friday, Saturday, and Sunday. Dustin Shane Smale was home when I knocked on the door, and was more than happy to tell me about the success of his pumpkin patch. "I just got this idea a few weeks ago. My uncle has a pumpkin farm, so I decided to try this business, too. I buy my pumpkins from him and pay him 50% of everything I sell. With my half I plan to put some of it into my college fund—I'm going to Notre Dame—and spend the other half on a new skateboard. The first weekend I made $252, and I have two more weekends to go before Halloween!" By the way, Dusty is ten years old.

Dusty Smale's Plan for a Successful Pumpkin Patch

1. Plan ahead several months in advance and plant pumpkin seeds according to the climate in your area. Check the seed packet for instructions. (Although this year he bought pumpkins from his uncle, next Halloween Dusty plans to cut his uncle out of the action by growing his own. Sharp!) Be sure you check with your parents before you plant; pumpkins have a tendency to spread out.

2. Make signs to advertise your sale. Hang them so that they can be seen by cars driving down your street. Talk to the kids at school and tell them to bring their parents by.

3. Go and check out the competition to decide your prices. Don't underprice, don't overprice, just charge about the same as the local grocery store does.

4. Wait for customers. Dusty's hours were Friday from 3 p.m. until dark, and then all day Saturday and all day Sunday. Be sure to keep your dogs out of the yard; they might scare people away. Don't let your friends hang around and talk to you, and don't ignore customers when they come. Be polite. Sit at the table as much as possible; don't let people see you playing in the yard. When people drive by, look them in the eye and they might stop and buy something. "If you are under 14, look at them kinda' pitiful and puppy-dog-like and they will probably feel bad and stop. And people give kids tips, too! I made $50 in tips last weekend!"

Dusty doesn't plan to put his business sense on hold until next Halloween; he is already making plans to make Christmas ornaments to sell in December. Notre Dame, watch out!

Educating Yourself

To learn more about growing pumpkins, you might want to check out this book:

The Pumpkin Book
Pumpkin Press
Box 139
Shasta, California 96087
$6.70 postpaid

Cookie Business

Jill Sheiman started baking cookies on a big scale when she was 13. Her first goal was simply to bake enough cookies to donate to a homeless shelter, but the scope of her project grew quickly and today, at 17, she is the president of her own nationwide cookie company. Jill's One Smart Cookie is a mail-order cookie success, and as a result of her business Jill has been featured in newspapers, magazines, and on television around the world. She was even on the "The Tonight Show" with Jay Leno; he wolfed down seven of Jill's cookies during the program!

When Jill told her family that she wanted to start a business they said "Fine, but you've got to run it like a grown-up, none of this kid stuff." And she does run it like a grown-up, testing her products in focus groups to see which are the most popular, doing all of her own investigation to find a bakery to custom-bake her products, and overseeing the order processing and filling of the mail orders. She does get one extra bit of help from her father; he is an attorney and so her legal advice is free.

Ideas for Financial Success in the Cookie Business

1. Start a neighborhood after-school "milk n' cookies" service for other kids whose parents are at work and unable to greet them at home in the afternoon with a plate of just-baked cookies. Arrange with their parents to come by at a particular time every day with a plate of six freshly made cookies (oatmeal raisin or chocolate chip are of course the two best bets) and a small carton of cold milk. This will serve two different purposes: parents can rest easy knowing that a responsible older child will be dropping in on their latch-key children to check on them, and they can also feel good about someone providing their children with such a warm and loving old-fashioned

treat. Sort of a combination babysitter/cook. Don't stay too long at each house though; you don't want to leave your next customers watching out the window wondering when their cookies will arrive!

2. A solid one-time money raising idea to start your camp fund, or save up for a new computer, is to hold your own one-day bake sale. You can set up your stand in front of your own house if the neighborhood traffic will warrant it, or approach your church or local neighborhood store about setting up there. Be honest and upfront about the fact that the money will benefit you personally. Chances are that the person in charge will be impressed that you have the ambition to earn this money on your own instead of just expecting your parents to provide.

3. On a somewhat larger scale than the milk n' cookies service is the idea of alerting the neighborhood to your incredible baking talents and offering your services to provide large batches of homemade cookies. Everyone needs a few dozen homemade cookies once in awhile, whether to bring to the office on "goodie day," send to school with their children for a bake sale, or to serve at a birthday party. Not every parent has the time or the inclination to bake nowadays.

Never underestimate the public's interest in a good chocolate chip cookie! What has worked in a big way for Mrs. Fields, Famous Amos, and young Jill Sheiman can also make extra money for you. When deciding prices for these ideas, don't forget to take the costs of materials (flour, eggs, sugar, and so forth) into account to make certain that you are earning a handsome profit on your tasty goods.

Fanzines

Fanzines, or 'zines as the truly hip call them, are small, inexpensively produced underground newspapers and magazines devoted to just about anything that you can be a fan of. Surfing, snowboarding, a particular rock band or musical style, a type of computer, or even a video game. At 17, Zach Meston of Hawaii started a fanzine devoted to video games on the Amiga computer. Devotees of the Amiga computer were loyal and fanatic (and convinced that the Amiga was vastly superior to anything else on the market), and Zach's 'zine was a success from the start.

Unlike giveaway newspapers, 'zines make their money primarily through subscriptions. Fans want to read about their topic of interest, usually one that is not given much space in the traditional media, so a fanzine is the only way to read about it. Who ever heard of the Seattle grunge scene until Nirvana made a hit record and the *New York Times* started to send reporters out? Why, readers of music 'zines like *Maximum Rock n' Roll* and *Teen Meat* knew all along what was happening.

Getting Started

You must have a passionate interest in an unusual topic to make a fanzine work. Zach was passionate about the Amiga and was able to pass that along to his loyal readers. What are you passionate about? If you and your friends are passionate about something that is underreported in the mainstream media you might have the basis for a successful 'zine. First do a quick survey among your friends to make sure that there isn't already another 'zine available. If there is, well then maybe you can do it even better!

Fanzines are notoriously inexpensive to produce. Turn on your computer, or put paper in your typewriter, and go. Take what you produce down to the corner copy shop and have them run off as many black and white copies as you need. And that is about it—no fancy artwork, no expensive photography or glossy printing. Your readers want hard-to-get information, not art.

Finding Customers

For your initial subscribers you should turn to the other fans that you know and ask for their help in spreading the word. If you are producing a music-related 'zine, approach your local record store and ask them to stock it on a "consignment" basis in the magazine rack. This means that they will only pay you for the issues that sell, so there is no financial risk to them in carrying your 'zine. With a computer 'zine, approach the local computer stores in the same way. Once you have built up your subscription and circulation base and established yourself you might also return to those same stores as a potential advertiser!

Zach's Door

Zach's advice for anyone trying to get into a particular business—"If they won't let you in the door, just make your own door!" And that is exactly what he did with his Amiga gaming magazine. Now, at age 21, he is a contributing editor to a major gaming magazine ("They pay me good fundage!" he laughs), the author of several video game books, and also a game reviewer for many other magazines. He receives free copies of all the latest games in the mail for review, and is also well-paid for what he writes for the "pro-zines." So if you plan it right, your 'zine could very well be the start of your adult career.

Free Neighborhood Newspaper

More than one successful publisher got their start early in life by founding a small neighborhood newspaper. Why not put together a give-away newspaper or newsletter that covers the news in your own little area—family news or births and deaths, graduations, marriages, and successes. Big time newspapers seem only to cover crime and disaster nowadays; if you provide your neighborhood with an upbeat little newssheet you will be a great success.

Getting Started

Approach local businesses about advertising to get the money to produce your newspaper, and also to ensure that you make a profit. Sit down first and figure out exactly how much it will cost to print, and then figure out how much advertising you will have to sell to make it work. Don't charge too much, you would be wise to investigate the advertising prices of local newspapers and publications before you set your own. These prices may range from several hundred dollars to just a few; a reasonable starting point would be $20 for a small business ad.

With a home computer you can easily desktop publish your newspaper, but an old-fashioned typewriter will work just as well. If there is no computer at home, perhaps you can arrange to use a computer at school during afterhours. Talk to your teacher about your project and you might even get extra credit for it! To start with you should write and produce a small folded paper that would allow you to have just two or four pages to fill. Once your circulation (the number of copies that you distribute) grows and you attract more advertisers, then you can produce a larger newspaper.

Finding Customers

One great pool of potential advertisers would be other neighborhood kids who want to advertise the special entrepreneurial services that they provide, things like babysitting, lawn raking, and dog walking. Don't charge kids as much for advertising as you would a full-fledged neighborhood business; $5 to $10 an ad for a kid's ad is enough. Their parents might also be potential advertisers for garage and yard sales or used furniture that they'd like to sell.

Ideas for Topics and Stories for Your First Issue

1. School sports. Wins, loses, new team members, upcoming games, and schedules of fundraising events are all important to potential readers.

2. New additions to the neighborhood. These could be babies, newly arrived residents, or even new buildings, houses, and businesses. New businesses would be

especially pleased to be featured in a neighborhood newspaper, and you might have discovered a new advertiser, too!

3. Neighborhood organizations. Crime watch programs, local political groups, and booster groups are interested in letting the rest of the neighborhood know what you are doing.

4. Family profiles. Meet your neighbors! Choose one family every month and write an interesting profile that talks about each member of the family.

Arik's Environmental Plug

Arik Trebnik had a monthly neighborhood newspaper in Indianapolis that talked about neighborhood environmental issues like the pending closure of the local landfill. He did not have advertising in his paper, only plugs for his own recycling pick-up service! "It was a great way to get customers, I made tons of money!" he told me. "I tied a wagon to the back of my bike and rode around the neighborhood picking up cans and newspapers to sell at the recycling center." Arik was 12 at the time; he has since gone on to become a teenage computer whiz.

Educating Yourself

When writing your stories, also remember the basic rules that newspaper reporters everywhere follow, that every story must contain who, what, where, why, and how. Who did it? What happened? Where did it happen? Why did it happen? How did it happen? If you keep those questions in mind when writing, your readers will always clearly understand what you have written. Now go out and get the story! Here is a great source of information:

Make Your Own Newspaper
Chris and Ray Harris
Bob Adams Publishing
$9.95

Recycling Pick-up Service

In *Free Neighborhood Newspaper* I mentioned Arik Trebnik and his neighborhood environmental newspaper. He developed, wrote, and distributed the newspaper as a way of getting the word out about his real business—a recycling pickup service. Naturally, the things that he picked up he would haul into the redemption center for real money! Over the course of one summer he earned $400 by operating this business. Developing a recycling pickup service in your own neighborhood performs a real service not only to your bank account, but also to your neighbors and the environment.

Getting Started

There is no charge to your customers. You simply establish a convenient time to stop by and pick up their recyclables and make your money when you turn the items in to your local recycling center. Investigate beforehand to find out what type of recyclable material is redeemable. Typically, you can get money back for bringing in the following:

> aluminum cans
> glass (separate by colors)
> newspapers
> cardboard
> plastic milk and juice bottles

Redemption policies and cash values will vary from region to region and state to state; there is no set national standard. However, if you discover that newspapers, for instance, will not bring any money back, you should continue to pick them up from your customers as a courtesy to them. If you bring that added benefit to their attention they may well appreciate the service enough to tip you.

Finding Customers

Arik's idea about the free environmental newspaper is a great way to get customers. So is using a simple flyer that you can make up and distribute from door to door. Once your customers start to brag about what a simple and handy free service you provide, others are certain to want to join in as clients.

In addition to establishing a pickup route in your neighborhood you might also want to keep a sharp eye out for extra sources of recyclables. One of Arik Trebnik's favorite sources were construction sites. "Construction workers get real thirsty throughout the day and they drink a lot of soda. It is a gold mine of aluminum cans after they go home at night!" However, you cannot just walk onto a construction site and start picking up things; the owners will become very, very nervous. Go and introduce yourself to the boss first and let him or her know what you have in mind. Once you receive permission you can really clean up! Neighborhood parks and picnic sites are also ideal, as is any place where crowds of thirsty people are likely to gather.

Redeeming recyclables is not a fast way to make a buck, but it can provide a great steady source of extra pocket money while at the same time contributing a real community service.

Swimming Pool Maintenance

Does your family have a swimming pool in the backyard? If so, you probably play a pretty big role in keeping it maintained—vacuuming the bottom for hours on the weekends, turning that handle over and over to backflush, and skimming leaf after leaf from the surface. You know all the ins and outs. Why not put that knowledge to work and rent yourself out as a swimming pool maintenance person on the weekends and after school? Clint Eastwood started as a pool guy, and look where he is today!

Getting Started

To start a pool service you should first decide how much extra time you have available. It may be that you will only have enough extra time on the weekends to take care of one or two clients at the most. Don't forget how time-consuming it is to take care of a pool. What teenager wants to spend every free hour bending over a swimming pool? You should figure on at least two solid hours per pool, if not more.

As you go from pool to pool, you will not be bringing equipment with you, but rather using what is available at your client's home. Pool-cleaning equipment is very expensive; treat it with care and respect. Discuss the chlorine and chemicals issue with your customer in advance. They may prefer to add their own chemicals. Do not volunteer to add chemicals unless you are truly knowledgeable and have been dealing with the chemicals in your own family's pool for several years.

It is also important to discuss with your client how often certain maintenance tasks should be performed. Some people will only want their pool vacuumed once a month and skimmed carefully every week; others may prefer more frequent vacuuming. You and your client both need to agree on what your weekly and monthly tasks will be in order to prevent any misunderstanding.

Setting Rates

To set your rates you should be familiar with what other pool services charge. Phone around to get a few estimates, and then set your rates below theirs. The best way to get clients is to let your friends know that you will be doing this on the weekends. You can be sure that, if they have pools, they will happily spread the word to their parents in the hopes that it will excuse them from the job!

Vacation Housewatching Service

Every summer most folks in your neighborhood go on vacation for a week or two, and every last one of them is in need of an honest and reliable teenager to take care of their house while they are gone. Vacationers have a much better time relaxing if they know that there is someone in their own neighborhood who will stop by once or twice a day to take care of things. You can become that person and earn extra summer cash by establishing your own vacation housewatching service!

The most important thing that you can offer your customers is a feeling of safety. Burglars keep a sharp eye out for homes that look vacant. A yellowing newspaper on the front lawn and an outdoor light on in the middle of the afternoon are sure signs that no one is around and the coast is clear to stage a burglary. As a vacation housewatcher it is your responsibility to make sure that your client's house has a "lived-in" look at all times.

Services You Can Offer Vacationing Homeowners

1. Bring in the newspaper every day while they are out of town. It is important to do this in the morning. If the newspaper sits out all day long it will be noticed by the wrong people.

2. Water the lawn as needed. Depending on how long your clients will be gone, you might not have to water the lawn, or you might have to do it several times.

3. Water indoor and outdoor plants as needed. Outdoor plants in pots need to be kept fresh looking in order to maintain the "lived-in" look, and indoor plants need as much water as their owners instruct.

4. Feed and care for animals if necessary. Many travelers will board their animals during a long vacation, but aquarium fish still need feeding! Be sure to read the section on animal sitting elsewhere in this book so that you understand all of the issues involved.

5. Bring in the mail on a daily basis. It is important to arrange beforehand with your client whether it is important that the mail be kept in the order of the day it was received or just lumped together all in one big jumble. Make sure that it is in an easy-to-find place

and that the stack does look neat. No one wants to return home after a long trip and either not be able to find their mail at all, or find it strewn all over the front hall. You should also bring in any advertising flyers, circulars, or business cards that are left on the front porch. Don't leave these things lying around out front.

6. Turn the lights on at night. Some folks might want only their porch light turned on; others might want an interior light or two turned on every so often to make it look as though someone really is at home. Discuss this very carefully with your clients so that you understand exactly what they expect of you. Lights that are turned on at night will, of course, need to be turned off in the morning when you bring in the newspaper.

Finding Clients

It will be difficult to approach strangers with a business idea like this, so start off by alerting the neighbors you know best that you will be offering this service. Once you have established yourself you can ask for referrals to their friends. This is a business for a very responsible person, so be honest with yourself about whether you want to take on a big job like this.

Thinking It Through

If you decide to start a small business you must make every effort to follow through on your promises. Adopt a responsible and adult outlook toward your business and you will be developing habits that will serve you your whole life. Here are some hard questions that you should ask yourself before you undertake a business:

1. Are you responsible enough? Be truthful when answering this. There is no point in starting a business in which other people will be counting on you to follow through (like a vacation service, or a pool service) if you cannot handle the responsibility. Better to start small with one-shot ideas like a bake sale than to take on more than you can handle right now.

2. Can you handle money wisely? Talk to your parents about what it will mean if you start to make money on your own. Will they discontinue your allowance or expect you to put it all in a savings account for the future? You will also need to talk to them about paying taxes, depending on how much money you make you may have to file an income tax return every year. Now that is a BIG responsibility!

3. Do you have the extra time to run a business? Don't start a business that will take time away from your school hours, your homework, or any sports or extracurricular activities that you are involved in. Having a business should be fun, not burdensome. A wonderful side benefit to having a business in your teens is that it can go a long way toward helping you get into the college of your choice. Admissions officers are always impressed by personal drive and ambition, and what better way to display that than the fact that you operated your own business?

Educating Yourself

This chapter only scratches the surface of ideas for teen businesses. Two great books to read for more ideas are:

> *Kids Can Make Money Too!*
> *How Young People Can Succeed Financially, with Over*
> *200 Ways to Earn Money and Make It Grow*
> Vada Lee Jones
> Calico Paws Publishing
> P.O. Box 2364
> Menlo Park, CA 94026
> (415) 323-9616
> $9.95

> *Better Than a Lemonade Stand: Seventy-five Small Business Ideas for Kids*
> Daryl Bernstein
> Beyond Words Publishing
> $7.95

Chapter Five

Crafty Business— Money-Making Ideas for Crafts Fairs

Crafts and hobbies have kept many of us happy and busy throughout the years. With the crafts craze sweeping the nation nowadays, selling the crafts we make can also keep us happily going to the bank to make hefty deposits! Detailed in this chapter are exciting ways to make money selling crafts at fairs, bazaars, boutiques, and markets, as well as through mail-order catalogs, gift shops, and department stores. If you already make crafts now, think about kicking your hobby into a higher gear and turning it into a SAM. And if you don't have a craft or hobby already, take at look at some of the options here, choose one, and start making money as fast as you can make your products!

Birdhouses and Bird Feeders

You may have read that Americans are going through a phase called "nesting," where instead of going out on the town in pursuit of pleasure they are staying put on the couch watching videos and reading books, working around the house, and just generally enjoying the quiet life. This "nesting" movement has also inspired an interest in our feathered friends, the wild birds. Nature walks to observe birds are a big deal, sales of binoculars and field guides are way up, and everyone wants a beautiful custom-made birdhouse or bird feeder hanging outside their window. This is an ideal time to put your woodworking and designing skills to work and start your own weekend birdhouse business.

Birdhouses and bird feeders come in all sizes, shapes, and materials. Some entrepreneurs make them from recycled scrap wood, others use foraged materials from the woods to create a more outdoorsy look. One northern California crafter covers the exteriors of her handmade birdhouses with the seedpods from pinecones. A popular design technique is to custom-build a birdhouse that is a miniature copy of the homeowner's own abode, even painted to match!

Finding Customers

There are many ways to market handcrafted birdhouses and bird feeders. Crafts fairs are the natural place to start, but keep in mind that most folks who shop at crafts fairs like items in the under $5 range. During one afternoon crafts fair I hung up a Frank Lloyd Wright-inspired bird feeder that my husband Peter had built. At $60 it had plenty of admirers but no actual purchasers. If you plan to sell your wares at a crafts fair it is best to experiment with fairly simple designs that you can sell cheaply and still make a profit.

To sell high-priced birdhouses and feeders a better method is to approach the merchandise buyer at one of the many nature or outdoor-theme stores that are cropping up all over. Offer your product to the store at a wholesale price (approximately 50% of what you think it will sell for retail) or ask if they will handle it on consignment. With a consignment arrangement you will be paid only when the bird feeder sells, but you can expect to keep a little more than 50%. Ambitious woodworkers with more capital to invest might try advertising their custom birdhouses or feeders in regional lifestyle magazines like *Sun-*

set or *Southern Living*, but the cost of display advertising is high and this is a risky method for a beginner.

Educating Yourself

Once you begin building birdhouses and bird feeders you will find that your designs will grow more and more imaginative, but to get started with ideas you might take a look at these two books:

> *The Bird House Book*
> *How to Build Fanciful Bird Houses and Feeders, from the*
> *Purely Practical to the Absolutely Outrageous*
> Bruce Woods and David Schoonmaker
> Sterling/Lark
> $19.95

> *The Bird Feeder Book*
> *How to Build Unique Bird Feeders from the Purely Prac-*
> *tical to the Simply Outrageous*
> Thom Boswell
> Sterling/Lark
> $19.95

Cats and Kittens

We all love our pets, and cat lovers sometimes seem to be the most devoted of all. Not only do they lavish love and attention on their cats, but they also spend big bucks on cat and kitten-oriented merchandise. There are even retail stores around the country that carry nothing but items for cat fanciers. Weekend entrepreneurs might find that making cat-related crafts is a purr-fect way to make extra money!

Crafters can make a wide variety of cat and kitten-inspired merchandise. Quilted cat dolls dressed in clothing, needlepoint and embroidered wall hangings, painted wood or stone doorstops (take a look at *Foraging the Wild* in Chapter 3 for a great idea here!), t-shirts and sweatshirts painted with cat designs, pet portraits, and even custom-made cat toys and feeding bowls are just a few ideas that crafters can develop and sell. If there is a retail store in your town that specializes in all things feline, you should visit and acquaint yourself with the merchandise already on the market. Perhaps you have found a potential customer for your kitty wares! *Cat Fancy* magazine caters to serious devotees of purebred cats, but it also has many advertisements for merchandise that will give you creative ideas. "Christmas cats" are hot—little kitties with Santa hats and furry faces peeking out of green felt stockings, ornaments, and other hanging decorations are snapped up at crafts fairs during the holiday season.

Finding Customers

The best way to sell this type of merchandise at a weekend crafts fair is to offer a wide variety of merchandise at your booth. Instead of a small booth that only offers painted Victorian wooden cats, for instance, why not convince a few other crafters to produce cat-related crafts and sell their wares at your booth as well? You will increase everyone's odds of having a successful fair. Once you establish yourself as a cat-craft entrepreneur you might want to investigate the weekend cat show circuit. Cat shows happen all over the country every weekend and the shows always have booths with high-priced merchandise. This is a much more serious and expensive undertaking than selling at crafts fairs, but if you decide that this is the perfect business for you it is worth checking out.

Chile Wreathes and Other Southwestern Crafts

The heart of the Southwest, Santa Fe, New Mexico, was just voted the number one favorite travel destination in the United States by the readers of *Conde Nast Traveler,* and southwestern-theme crafts continue to travel off the shelves in a big way too! To cash in on this mania for southwestern merchandise here are two different ways that you can try.

Chile Ristras and Wreathes

Chile ristras are long strings of red or green chile peppers that cooks like to hang in their kitchens for decoration or for a handy ingredient. You can make inexpensive chile ristras yourself by first growing chile peppers (very easy to grow!) and then stringing them together on heavy duty fishing line. Wreathes are also easy to make with chiles, and very popular items not only at Christmas but year round too. Other interesting chile-related Christmas crafts are miniature trees made from chiles, and long swags of greenery decorated with chiles for accent color. Sharon Geier of Fairfield, California does a steady business at her local craft collective with her raffia and chile swags.

Coyote Cutouts

The "trickster" coyote is another potent and popular symbol of the Southwest, and standing wooden coyotes are perennial crafts fair favorites. To find a good pattern, flip through southwestern magazines and design magazines until you find the silhouette of the howling coyote. Enlarge it on a copy machine and voilà, you have a pattern to use for wooden cutouts. Coyotes can be window decorations, doorstops, hanging ornaments, and whatever else strikes your fancy. One enterprising weekend entrepreneur markets mailbox flags of the howling coyote! Paint the coyotes in southwestern desert colors, lots of turquoise, sand, faded pink, and sunset orange.

Educating Yourself

Quilts, tea cozies, and oven mitts with a southwestern theme are also popular crafts fair items. You might find your needle and thread inspired by this book:

Contemporary Southwestern Quilts: A Practical Guide to
Developing Original Quilt Designs
Mary Evangeline Dillon
Chilton
$14.95

Custom Window Coverings
with Matching Bedspreads
and Quilts

Although she started by sewing "anything!" after two years in business Jaydine Rendall has found the perfect way to make extra money—sewing custom window treatments. "My grandmother taught me to sew; it really is a lost art nowadays. When I decided to stay home with the kids I investigated many different part-time businesses, everything from Avon, to typing, to computer stuff. But I decided to turn to what I knew, sewing. I'm able to work six to ten hours a week, and I average about $20 an hour for my time. It's a great home-based business for a mom!"

Conducting the Business

Jaydine had made her own valances years before, but to brush up on her technique she bought a book on sewing window treatments. She runs an advertisement in the Yellow Pages under "Window Dressing," and that one ad brings her enough business to stay as busy as she'd like. "January and February are pretty slow months; I get to spend more time with my kids. In the spring there seem to be lots of new baby's rooms that need custom curtains, and in the fall everyone goes crazy trying to spruce up their house for the holidays." The demand for curtains for new baby rooms has also developed into another service that Jaydine offers, custom bedspreads and pillows to match the curtains.

The customer buys the fabric and brings it to Jaydine's home. She then has an in-depth consultation to learn what kind of a look the customer wants to achieve. "Not everyone is easy to work with," she warns. "Some people are just never pleased, and if I sense that during our first meeting I will tell them that I can't do the job. I am busy enough that I don't have to take jobs from difficult people. That is one of the benefits of working for yourself; you can choose your clients carefully." During the initial meeting Jaydine asks for a 50% deposit up front, with full payment due upon completion.

Educating Yourself

A southern California woman who has operated several successful sewing businesses has written a book to help other sewing entrepreneurs begin:

> The "Business" of Sewing:
> How to Start, Maintain, and Achieve Success
> Barbara Wright Sykes
> Collins Publications
> (800) 247-6553
> $14.95

Friendly Plastic Jewelry

"Friendly plastic" is an extraordinarily simple-to-use, inexpensive, and versatile crafting material. Jewelry made from friendly plastic sells briskly at crafts fairs and in specialty shops, particularly around the holidays when Christmas-theme earrings and pins are popular. "I make enough money in the month before Christmas to buy all of the gifts for my family," one friendly plastic crafter bragged. "All I do is bring samples to the office with me, leave them on my desk in view of everyone who walks by, and take orders and checks. It's great!"

Friendly plastic is so inexpensive that the profit margin is high. Checking a local craft supply store in my neighborhood, I found a selection of 30 different colors on sale, two 7-inch strips for $1.49. Out of the strips it would be possible to make several pairs of earrings that could be sold for $6 to $10 retail.

Friendly plastic comes in very fashionable metallic colors. The earrings themselves can look quite hip or simply elegant depending on the style you make. Crafts stores also carry the earring wires, pierced backs, and pin backs you will need to finish the jewelry.

Crafting with friendly plastic is simple—cut the design and shape you'd like, stack the plastic in an attractive way, and pop it into an oven heated to 225° to 250° F for one minute or so. The heat from the oven fuses the plastic together and gives it a nice full look. Once the warmed plastic is removed from the oven you can also press small beads, sequins, or glitter into the design. Booklets on working with friendly plastic are available wherever craft supplies are sold.

Studying the Market

Before you launch your weekend career as a friendly plastic jewelry designer, you should first scout out your neighborhood to see what other crafters are making. Since it is an easy material to work with it is also very popular, and you do not want to simply duplicate what other crafters are making. Look at local gift stores to see if they carry the work of other crafters. Beauty parlors also sometimes stock handmade earrings near the cash register. Southern California crafter Kim Trujillo wore a pair of her own earrings while getting a haircut. By the time the hairdresser was finished with Kim's hair she had ordered 100 pairs to sell in the shop!

Furniture and Garden Accessories

"Well, I guess you could say my wife got me started. She saw a bench that she liked in an issue of *Country Living* magazine and then she kept after me for years to make it. I finally did, and that bench got so many compliments and requests from our friends and neighbors that I started making them for sale." Don Ballard laughed as he described his woodworking SAM to me.

"Those benches live on porches all over the country now, and I get a big kick out of that."

For the past three years, Don, a contractor by profession, has been making benches, windmills, whirligigs, and angels in his woodshop at home and selling them to friends and at crafts fairs. All of his products have a "country" feel to them. He believes that most people who decorate with the country style are seeking a warmer, more welcome atmosphere, and, "my bench sitting on the front porch surely does look welcome!"

Special Touches Sell Best

Don makes his wooden benches out of different grades of pine. The most expensive bench is $180, made from high-grade clear pine, but he does sometimes use less expensive wood to deliver a less-expensive finished product. "Most of my benches are sold through word-of-mouth; they are really too expensive to sell at crafts fairs. When I do crafts fairs I try to have as many items under $10 as possible, lots of rubber-band revolvers, small Christmas angels, and toy windmills. At $180 I hardly ever sell the benches."

Unique designs sell the best, he advises. Although his bench was inspired by a picture in a magazine, he modified it quite a bit, shortening the legs so that women's legs will touch the ground and angling the back to make it more comfortable to sit in. "That's what people are looking for, the special touch that they can't find at a furniture store."

Studying the Market

Woodworkers considering selling their wares should first consider the market. "Check out a bunch of crafts fairs to see what is already out there and how much it costs. And the most important thing to think about," Don warns, "is whether this is how you want to spend all of your free time. I enjoy my woodworking and I spend my spare hours in my woodshop producing things to sell. But not everybody wants to spend their time that way."

Educating Yourself

A good beginner's book on this topic is:

> *Building Outdoor Furniture*
> Percy W. Blanford
> Tab Books
> $15.95

Hand-Rolled Beeswax Candles

My success as a candle maker began with an innocent remark from my Auntie Bee, "Oh Jennifer, have I ever taken you to the little candle shop in Carmel?" Auntie Bee (and yes, this is her real name) had discovered a small shop on Ocean Avenue that sold flat sheets of beeswax that can be rolled into several sizes and shapes of candle. One five-minute lesson in rolling candles and I was immediately hooked. For years I made these beeswax candles just to give away as gifts at birthdays, Christmas, and housewarmings. But as I began to notice just how much these candles sold for in gift shops and through mail-order catalogs, my generous attitude changed. Their retail prices were several times what it cost me to make mine and I soon realized that I could easily sell my hand-rolled candles and undercut their prices. A weekend business was born!

I buy the flat sheets of colored beeswax from several sources, depending on which colors they stock. Not all of the suppliers carry all of the colors, and throughout the year my customers' whims change. Red and green sell well at Christmas; brown, dark wine, and other warm colors sell during Thanksgiving;, and pastels sell well in summer. I offer three different sizes—6-inch tapers, 12-inch tapers, and a thick and handsome long-burning 6-inch centerpiece candle. Each candle takes only 30 seconds or so to produce; an evening spent rolling candles while watching television can produce enough candles to last throughout a typical afternoon crafts fair. My wholesale cost for the wax sheets and the wicks (the only two elements required) averages around $1. From each sheet I can either produce two 8-inch high tapers, or one single long 16-inch taper. My retail prices for hand-rolled beeswax candles are:

two 6-inch tapers $4.50 (cost $1; profit $3.50)

two 12-inch tapers $8 (cost $2; profit $6)

four 6-inch tapers $8 (cost $2; profit $6)

one 6-inch long-burning centerpiece candle $10 (cost $2; profit $8)

My husband, Peter, a dedicated woodworker, has added to my wares by producing redwood candle holders from recycled redwood and left-over odds and ends from his other projects. I sell one of the short, thick candles in a redwood candle holder, decorated with a small seasonal wreath or an elegant silk ribbon bow, for $12. The finished candles are sold primarily at local crafts fairs and holiday bazaars, but I also do a brisk business among my coworkers at Christmas time.

A Typical Sales Day

To give you a sense of what a typical afternoon of sales is like, here is a quick report on sales at my booth at the Granite Bay Christian Preschool First Annual Crafts Fair in the month of November:

I arrived at 8 a.m., per the instruction sheet that I had been mailed. My booth space was just inside the doorway in a converted kindergarten room. Dragging my folding teak table from the back of the car, I began to build my candle display. I have a rather elaborate look that I try to duplicate every time that I sell at a crafts fair. My theory is that you should try to make your potential customers want your products because they want the "lifestyle" that you are portraying. To achieve that end I create a tabletop display that would rival any Bloomingdale's Christmas window—gleaming antique silver candlesticks, soft linen table cloth, carefully arranged beeswax candles tied in pairs with gold silk ribbons, cut crystal bowls filled with dried flowers (also for sale, and foraged of course!). I also have a large standing screen covered with rich looking fabric to place behind the table and direct the eye toward my beautiful wares. Can't leave anything to chance.

My space at the crafts fair cost $30, so I would not begin to make my $100 goal until I passed my first $30. Open to the public at 10:00, I edged above $30 by 11:30. Throughout the day I had steady sales, but I also lost many other sales due to an error in judgment on my part—I had failed to anticipate the fact that Christmas colors would be in demand before Thanksgiving. If only I had brought another dozen pair of RED candles!! My total take for the day was $119, working from 8 a.m. until the fair closed at 4 p.m. Not the best ever, but it gave me a clue to what customers would be looking for the following weekend at a larger fair I was attending. I packed my car with my display and my unsold candles and headed straight for the beekeeping supply store to buy as many sheets of red beeswax as I could!

Learning the Market

Not content to just tell you about my candle-selling experiences, I contacted another successful beeswax candle crafter to see what kind of advice she had for weekend entrepreneurs: "I have been selling handmade beeswax candles every other weekend at the Jack London Square Farmers' Market in Oakland for years," Pat Hill told me. "I used to offer both the basic cylinder type as well as the fancy spiral type, but since the spirals outsold the other by 2 to 1 I dropped that choice. I sell my spiral candles for $2 a pair and, combined with selling jars of our home-grown honey, I make anywhere from $300 to $600 a day. It is definitely worth my time!"

Educating Yourself

Learning how to make beeswax candles is not difficult. Check the class schedule at your local crafts store. Beekeeping supply stores are another good source; I have been able to purchase a broad range of materials at a beekeeping store in Sacramento, California. Once you find a source for the flat sheets of wax, check their prices and keep digging for other sources. Prices range from $1.90 per sheet to $1 per sheet, and the lowest price I have seen is 69¢ per sheet! The lower your cost for goods, the greater your profit on your products, so always be on the lookout for better sources. If you are unable to find a store in your area that carries the beeswax sheets, here are mail-order sources:

B&B Honey Farm (507) 896-3955

Candlewic Company (215) 348-9285

The A.I. Root Company (800) BUY-ROOT

Sacramento Beekeeping Supplies (916) 451-2337

I am already planning to add another product to my crafts fair offering next Christmas—scented beeswax Christmas tree ornaments. Naturally, I will sell them for under $5 to really maximize sales! I found a simple recipe that can be used with tin candy molds in this book:

Gifts from the Herb Garden
Emelie Tolley and Chris Mead
Clarkson Potter
$18.00

As you can see, despite the fact that the hot selling season is only from early October until just before Christmas, thinking about crafts fairs is a year-round preoccupation! The greater the selection and the more varied the merchandise, the better the chance that your sales will soar.

Patterns for Tole Painters

Tole painting is a popular craft, and Lisa Soderborg of Denver, Colorado, has found a terrific SAM as a result of her interest in it. "Tole painters are always looking for interesting wood patterns on which to paint, and I started making my own six years ago. Once my fellow tole painters found out that I could cut patterns, they started to come to me with pattern books asking me to make this shape or that shape. I didn't really sit down and plan this business; it just sort of happened!"

Lisa buys pine lumber in all different sizes and custom cuts it for her customers. As a full-time mom of two with another one on the way, she finds that her pattern-cutting business can easily be run in her spare time. "I go out to my shop and cut when the kids are in bed, or in school, whenever I have some extra time. It's a great stress reliever for a mother." After starting out with just a scroll saw, over the years Lisa has acquired more equipment. She now also owns a band saw, router, belt sander, drill press, palm sander, and a jigsaw. Not very glamorous, but good solid equipment that she feels confident and comfortable using.

Studying the Market

To set her prices for custom pattern cutting, Lisa always makes sure that she is getting at least $8 an hour for her time, and also passes the full cost of the wood along to the customer. Her busiest seasons are October through December, with an additional flurry of activity around Easter. Although Lisa limits her work to custom pattern cutting on demand, she does encourage other woodworkers to approach craft and hobby supply stores about carrying custom-designed patterns for tole painters. Do research at the stores and among crafters to learn what types of patterns are the most popular before beginning to create a product.

Porcelain Dolls and Christmas Ceramics

Full-time mom Cindy Davis has a flourishing weekend business creating porcelain dolls and custom ceramics. "I learned how to paint and fire the dolls from a woman in town who owned a doll shop. Once I felt confident enough to work on my own I bought a kiln and took it from there. Most towns have porcelain doll shops and ceramics stores. Just look in the Yellow Pages under "Dolls" or "Ceramics" to find one where you can take lessons." Even though Cindy works on her own at home to produce her wares, she still buys the basic unfired materials from the shops.

Her dolls are works of art. Cindy paints each one individually and handsews the clothing. Sold mostly through word of mouth, the dolls go for as much as $300. "Each one has its own personality; sometimes it is hard to sell them after I've worked on them so long. They are like my little babies!"

Ceramic Christmas trees are much easier to part with. Cindy buys the greenware from the ceramics shop and individually paints each tree before firing it in the kiln. She does a brisk business in the preholiday crafts fair season with her trees, selling the 16-inch model for as much as $60 and the smaller versions for $30 to $50. The more expensive trees include music boxes and blinking lights to add to the price. "I make a greater profit on the dolls than I do on the Christmas trees," Cindy admits, "but they sell much faster at the crafts fairs than the dolls do. The wholesale price on the undecorated trees is around $38, I make a $20 profit by the time I decorate and sell it."

Potpourri and Herbal Products

Working as a nurse and respiratory therapist in Anacortes, Washington, Darcy Tietjen has seen enough of what chemicals can do to our bodies. She started her own part-time potpourri and herbal products company, Proverbs 31 Woman, so that she could work with and sell all-natural products. "We moved into a new house that had 24 beautiful rose plants already well-established in the garden. I thought it would be such a waste to just throw the flowers away when they were through blooming. I bought a book to learn how to make pot-pourri and rose waters, and I was on my way!"

Proverbs 31 Woman

Darcy now has an extensive product line and sells her wares at crafts fairs and in local crafters' galleries and boutiques. Although her full line includes expensive items like rose waters and bath vinegars bottled in antique glass bottles, she always includes lower priced items in order to attract impulse gift shoppers. Small handmade soaps are priced under a dollar and are meant to be used as stocking stuffers or as an attractive topping for a wrapped package. She recommends that other crafters follow this same pricing philosophy.

After two years in business, Darcy is very choosy about just which crafts fairs she attends and who is putting them on. "It matters to me who the organizer is," she says. "The organizer and the kind of advertising and coverage they choose make a big difference in who attends. I really like church bazaars." Crafts shows take a lot of time on the weekends, Darcy warns. Friday and Saturday are the two biggest days. Craft boutiques and galleries are another outlet for her wares. She leaves them on consignment in several places throughout the county.

"This is not a business for dilettantes; if you are easily bored and start up many projects at once then this is not a business for you." She advises prospective potpourri makers and sellers to look long and hard at the future—if you really want to devote the time and effort this will take to succeed, then go for it. "It takes awhile to get established; there are real ups and downs, but it is worth it!"

Carmel Essence

In addition to Darcy's success, I'd like to share a business idea that I created several years ago for a cousin. His parents live in Carmel, and were more than a bit annoyed that their son, then a recent college graduate, was spending most of the summer hanging around the house doing nothing. "Hmmm . . . Carmel? Quaint little beach town with a steady supply of tourists? Do I have an idea for you!" I said, and here is what I outlined: Potpourri is big business, and in any kind of quaint tourist town there is the potential to capitalize on this scented craze. Forage for materials that are common to the area (in Carmel, for instance, I recommended eucalyptus leaves and seedpods, pine needles, and small seashells) to use as bulk in your potpourri, and then add the necessary scent. You will then have a product that will appeal to tourists who would like to take home a small, inexpensive souvenir, as well as a product that gift stores will be happy to stock. Design a nice package and you are on your way! "Carmel Essence" was easily created from foraged materials, but it could just as easily be "Tahoe Pines," "Oregon Forest," or "Carolina Coast." Help yourself to my idea, and do let me know how it works. My cousin never did follow up; he became a stockbroker instead.

Educating Yourself

How to get started making potpourris and other herbal products? There are several good books on the market that are filled with recipes, drying tips, and instructions. Unfortunately, they are primarily available in hardcover only, not paperback. "Books are probably my single biggest business expense," says Darcy. "Whenever I see a new one published I just have to pick it up and see if there is any new information I need." Before you decide to take the plunge into this type of a SAM you might want to see if your local library has books on this topic.

Once you are committed, by all means look for these books in your local bookstore:

> *The Scented Room*
> *Cherchez's Book of Dried Flowers, Fragrance, and Potpourri*
> Barbara Milo Ohrbach
> Clarkson N. Potter
> $18

> *The Complete Book of Nature Crafts*
> *How to Make Wreathes, Dried Flower Arrangements, Potpourris, Dolls, Baskets, Gifts, Decorative Accessories for the Home, and Much More*
> Eric Carlson, Dawn Cusick, and Carol Taylor
> Rodale Press
> $24.95

> *Potpourri . . .*
> *Easy as One, Two, Three*
> Dody Lyness
> Berry Hill Press
> 7336 Berry Hill
> Palos Verde, California 90274-4404
> $6.95

The Berry Hill Press also publishes *Potpourri Party-Line,* a quarterly designed to keep readers abreast of the floral trends. Every issue includes new recipes. Write for subscription information.

Finding wholesale suppliers is always difficult when starting any type of business. Many crafting magazines carry ads for potpourri suppliers, and here are a few:

> San Francisco Herb Company
> (415) 861-3018 or (800) 227-4530

> The Essential Oil Company
> free catalog
> (800) 729-5912
> in Oregon (503) 697-5992

Frontier Cooperative Herbs
Box 299
Norway, Iowa 52318
(319) 227-7996

To learn more about fast-selling homemade products like herbal vinegars and herbal oils there are two books that I recommend:

Gifts from the Herb Garden
Emelie Tolley and Chris Mead
Clarkson Potter
$18.00

The Herbal Pantry
Emelie Tolley and Chris Mead
Clarkson Potter
$18.00

Thinking It Through

America has gone crazy for crafts, and fairs and boutiques to fuel this passion have sprung up across the country. Crafters of all description are successfully displaying and selling their wares at these shows, but there are also crafters who sit alone and unappreciated at their booths because their wares are not quite up to snuff. Before you gear up to produce your crafts on a large scale take the time to give your product a critical look. Is it well made? Useful? Affordable? Unique? Ask your friends for an honest evaluation of your wares and pay attention to their suggestions. Don't be hurt if you fail to pass the scrutiny test. Consider how much time and effort you have just saved yourself! Go back to the drawing board for another idea.

Learning Your Craft

Most cities and towns have crafting classes available through a craft store, the local parks and recreation department, or private instruction. Take advantage of the knowledge available in these classes and who knows, perhaps once you master a craft and achieve success at the fairs you can then add to your profits by offering instruction!

The Business of Crafting

Almost every one of the crafters I spoke to returned again and again to the topic of pricing. Pricing your wares is a critical element for success—it is better to sell large quantities of low-priced items than to sell nothing at all because your products are too expensive. Try to detach your ego from the price tag.

Profit is another important element of success, and sometimes crafters have a difficult time approaching it in a businesslike manner. Because so many crafters started as hobbyists, it is sometimes difficult to develop a more professional attitude toward their weekend SAM. You should always try to make at least twice as much as you have paid for your supplies.

Like any other business in which your ego is on the line, you must be prepared to handle rejection. Many shoppers will walk by your booth, glance down at your beautiful handmade wares, and then just keep on walking. This can be a difficult experience to take, but if you have first tested the quality of your products among friends and relatives you can reassure yourself that what you are offering simply doesn't fit that person's need. Do not feel embarrassed and rejected every time someone fails to buy. Focus instead on the wonderful feeling that you get when someone does fawn over your products, buys out everything you have made, and then displays it in their home.

Educating Yourself

To keep your products current with the most popular trends it is important to read the crafting magazines on the market. Not only will you learn what is hot and new, but you will also run across idea after idea (along with instructions!) for more crafts to sell. Among the most popular crafting magazines available on newsstands are *Crafts 'n Things,* and *Country Handcrafts.* Once you decide to approach your hobby with a more business-like attitude it is a good idea to subscribe to the *Crafts Report.* This monthly tabloid is filled with interesting articles about professional crafters, lists very complete state-by-state information on upcoming crafts fairs, and is a good lead source for wholesale suppliers. A one-year subscription is $24; call them at (800) 777-7098.

Chapter Six

Odds and Ends— Great SAMs That Defy Categories

Some things in life just don't fit neatly into categories, and the weekend entrepreneurs in this chapter sure don't! Here are some wacky ideas, some silly ideas, and some downright strange ideas, but rest assured that these are all terrific SAMS. If you have the talent, the skills, or live in the sort of specialized area in which some of these business ideas will work, then get started immediately on these creative ways to make extra cash.

Designing and Leading Custom Tours

Bruce Kayton has an unusual knowledge about a seldom-seen side of New York City's districts and neighborhoods—he knows the history of "radical New York." For $6 he will lead you on a 2½ hour tour unlike any you have ever experienced, pointing out where Emma Goldman lived and Abbie Hoffman hid. In the past two years he has led over one thousand people on his walking tours of New York.

In San Francisco, Shirley Fong-Torres takes groups of up to 12 on gourmet food and shopping tours of the world famous

Chinatown area, stopping in to watch noodle factories at work and partake of Chinese delicacies.

Both of these quirky tour leaders base their success on a genuine interest and personal knowledge of their subjects and their good fortune to live in large cities rife with color, culture, and history. But you don't have to live in a big city to create and lead unusual tours. With a little imagination and a lot of research, you can come up with a tour idea that will work in your area.

Leading unique tours is a perfect SAM for a weekend entrepreneur—weekends are ideal for this kind of tour. However, this is not a SAM for shy people; to succeed as a tour leader you must feel comfortable talking in front of groups of people. A sense of humor won't hurt, either. Most walking tours should last between two and three hours, and tour prices should range from $5 to $10. Bruce Kayton sometimes draws 50 people for his Radical Tours, not a bad way to earn $300 in an afternoon.

Tour Ideas

There are endless possibilities for tour ideas. Live out in the country? Why not develop a guided tour of "U-Pick-It" farms and lead a group of food-loving city folk from farm to farm, berry picking and pea plucking, ending up in a great down-home restaurant. During the fall you could organize a driving tour of beautiful autumn leaves and colors. The countryside has history too; research the major events that have taken place over the years and develop an exciting and informative talk.

To get started in designing a specialized tour of your area, here are the best general topics. Study them and be creative about the special "twists" that you could give them in your town or area.

1. **Food.** Is your region known for a particular specialty food or regional cuisine? Fresh produce grown nearby or unique products manufactured? Lots of brew-pubs or small wineries in the area?

2. **History.** Literary history, battle sites, and even scandal have all been the basis for successful tours. In Los Angeles and in Paris, tours are given of "permanent residents," those famous folks who are found in graveyards!

3. **Scenery.** Fall leaves, unknown waterfalls, wildlife and bird-watching, and acres of flowering tulips are popular starting points.

4. **Art.** Outdoor sculpture, architectural details, and even unusual neon signs could work.

Become an Expert

Look around your city or region with a new perspective. What is there that is unusual and might be of interest to others? What about your own knowledge and interests—what topic do you know about that would interest a group of strangers willing to pay $5 each to learn? Knowledge is the key to success in developing an unusual tour and gaining a following. Shirley Fong-Torres of Wok Wiz advises that the "top-of-the-list requirement for success is to have great knowledge of your topic. You must have a love for the topic; the public can see right through you if you don't. I have a true love for the food and the history of Chinatown."

Once you find a quirky idea that you think will work, become an expert and learn all that you can about the topic. Practice giving your tour to your friends and family before you try to attract paying customers. When you have developed your expertise, designed your tour, and feel comfortable with your topic, you are ready to begin leading the tours.

Reaching Your Audience

Write a press release and send it out to the media. If your tour is unusual enough they will cover it. Free media coverage is always worth trying for and can really be a big boost. Many small newspapers have "events" sections in which you can list your tour. Once you have used up all avenues for free coverage, place small ads in newspapers and magazines that would interest the type of folks you are trying to attract. Shirley Fong-Torres advertises Wok Wiz in the regional magazine *BayFood,* certain to be read by the foodies that might take her tour. Advertise historic tours in the local museum newsletter, and try to reach art lovers through galleries. Be creative about reaching your audience. Once you have established a following, your satisfied tourists will begin to do your advertising for you! Tourists and locals alike will be interested in what you have to offer. A woman in San Francisco advertises her Walk Tours as being "for anyone who wants to be a San Franciscan for a day—or for old-time San Franciscans who just want to know more about their city."

Environmental and "New Age" Products

Our world is changing around us, and a concern for the environment is becoming more and more mainstream. We are also becoming more spiritually aware. These two movements, the environmental movement and the "New Age" movement, have spawned many successful weekend entrepreneurs.

Baggits

"For years I marveled at the way my wife's family exchanged their gifts. They have so many kids that every year at Christmas there are likely to be upwards of two hundred gifts under the tree. But after the gifts are exchanged there is no huge mountain of ripped wrapping paper and ribbon to throw away. As thrifty home-sewers they have devised a simple cloth and ribbon gift bag that can be used year after year. I was so impressed by this method that I wanted to introduce the whole world to the idea." And that is how full-time natural foods wholesaler Francis Hamilton of Grass Valley, California, founded his spare-time company, Baggits.

Baggits makes one thing and one thing only: cloth bags in different sizes and materials, designed to be used either to wrap gifts or to hold scented sachets and potpourris. Early on, Francis decided not to sell directly to the public, but rather to rely on small retailers throughout northern California. "I guarantee each retailer that carries Baggits an exclusive in their area. It's not fair to a small store if I offer my product all over town. Why should they carry it if their neighbor does too?" Many of his local accounts are consignment accounts which Francis services himself. His largest single account, however, is a mail-order catalog that specializes in environmentally friendly products.

The future is bright for environmentally friendly goods and services. "When the full cost of disposal is considered in the cost of the product to the consumer, then a lot more manufacturers will become environmentally friendly," Francis predicts. "Any product, any way of doing anything out there, can be done in a way that is better for the planet. I'd encourage anyone to try to develop a product like this. We'll all be better off in the long run!"

There are pitfalls to manufacturing and selling a product on a part-time basis, however. Baggits has grown as large as it can with the time and money that Francis can devote to it. "If my orders increased tremendously at this point, so would my capital demands. People should understand that production requires a fair amount of money up front and that increased success also means increased investment of time and money. Know what it is that you want to achieve, and make sure that you have enough time left in the day to do it!"

Keep your eyes open for ways in which the things around us could be done better, and you will take the first step toward developing an environmentally friendly product.

Dream Pillows

Have you stepped inside a "New Age" store lately? Many items sold in stores, through catalogs, and at outdoor fairs are made by New Age weekend entrepreneurs. Crystal wands, Indian drums, sage smudges, and many other such items are handcrafted at home to meet the growing demand for these things. "Herb-filled 'Dream Pillows' are the fastest-selling product that we have right now," says the manager of Native Scents in Taos, New Mexico. Herbal Dream Pillows are filled with lavender, mugwort, rose petals, white sage, hops, yerba santa, and assorted other herbs, and when placed under your regular pillow they are supposed to encourage deep sleep. Hand rolled and tied sage smudge bundles are used increasingly by alternative doctors, therapists, and body workers to purify the air and to attract positive and beneficial energies.

Terra Flora

Maggie Lee of Terra Flora has a part-time business catering to the growing interest in New Age products. Her company produces and sells a package of mixed herbs designed to be used in herbal steam baths and sweat lodges. She packages her herbs in biodegradable cellophane and ties them with hand-dyed, desert-toned raffia. Small instruction cards printed on recycled card stock are tucked under the raffia tie. Maggie's products sell well in the Southwest and she is working to expand her market across the country and into New Age stores in other states.

New Age Angels

Another big trend in the New Age market is an interest in angels. Yes, that's right, those guys and gals with halos and wings. Books about angels, greeting cards, art, dolls—anything with an angelic theme is moving off the shelf. Look around at what the market already offers and see if there is an angel-related product missing. Maybe you are just the weekend entrepreneur to make it soar!

Gift Baskets

Who had ever heard of a gift basket before a few years ago? Suddenly they are everywhere, under every Christmas tree and on the doorstep of every new real estate client. This is a competitive field, but if you can come up with unique ideas and products and offer your customers an unusual twist, there is still room for part-time gift basket entrepreneurs.

Bodacious Baskets

In Auburn, California, Christie McKinnon runs her part-time gift basket business, the Bodacious Basket Company, as a sideline to her cruise-only tour company. "With the tour business, my income tends to fluctuate greatly from month to month, so I look to the gift baskets to even things out." Christie got started by taking a class from the local Learning Exchange on "How to Make Gift Baskets for Profit." Following her teacher's advice, she now makes specialty baskets for all occasions—baby showers, New Year's, anniversaries, birthdays, weddings, romance, and using her travel background wisely, a "vacation in a basket." The vacation in a basket is generally ordered by one spouse to surprise another and includes champagne, airline or cruise tickets, and other travel goodies like suntan lotion, sunglasses, and wacky shorts. Christie's price range for her gift baskets is $20 to $200. Lower-priced baskets sell faster, of course; but for very special occasions the sky seems to be the limit (especially when airline tickets are added in!). Gourmet food products are very popular right now, and so are personal care products. Whatever the contents, gift baskets seem to be a welcome treat for the recipient and are growing in popularity.

Getting Started

Start-up costs are relatively low in the gift basket business, and Christie found a great way to lower them even further. "Instead of buying a hand-held shrink wrap machine for $400, I went to my local hardware store and bought one of those heat-gun paint peelers—works great!" Be aware that you must have a wholesale license to buy products for your baskets.

How many different types of gift baskets are there? Hundreds! What about a "bath basket," with bubble bath, body oil, sponges, and talcum powder? Or a "gourmet chef" basket, filled with spices, wire whisks, recipe cards, and a cookbook? "Afternoon Tea" is a great idea, too, filled with exotic teas, delicate china cups, and linen napkins. What about a "Classic Cinema" basket, filled with a few old black and white films, some popcorn, and a box of Good N' Plenty candy! Once you start creating a few gift baskets, the ideas will begin to flow.

Setting Rates

To determine the price of your gift basket, use the following formula: add up the wholesale cost of everything in the basket (don't forget to include the cost of the basket, too) and triple it. That will give you the retail price that you should charge to ensure a tidy profit. For instance, if the wholesale value of a basket and its contents is $15, you will retail that basket for $45. A quick $30 profit for you!

Finding Clients

Gift baskets can be marketed several ways. Christie put the word of her wares out among friends who work in large state office buildings and started to get customers right away. Some creative marketers in Michigan started promoting their gift baskets through home parties styled like Tupperware parties. Linking up with real estate agents, insurance agents, large corporations, or anyone who regularly sends gifts to clients yields a terrific source of steady business.

Gift basket businesses are frequently touted as one of the hottest-growing businesses in the 90s. That means increased competition. Before you begin a part-time gift basket business, you should first check to see if there is any competition in your area. If there are already gift basket services available, decide whether you can offer something different. If you can, go for it!

Educating Yourself

The gift basket industry has grown in the last few years and now has an industry magazine and an annual trade show. The magazine, *Gift Basket Review,* is filled with inspirational stories about successful gift basket marketers, as well as advertisements for wholesale suppliers who cater to the gift basket industry.

> *Gift Basket Review*
> Festivities Publications
> $29.95 annual subscription
>
> *Building a Better Gift Basket Business*
> Festivities Publications
> $59.95
>
> The Gift Basket Video Series
> Festivities Publications
> $39.95 each
>
> Festivities Publications
> 1205 West Forsyth Street
> Jacksonville, FL 32204
> (904) 634-1902

Wholesale basket sources:

> Willow Specialties
> The Rochester Basket Company
> (800) 724-7300
>
> Palecek Picnic Baskets
> (800) 274-7730
>
> Dearan Imports, Inc.
> (619) 530-2212
>
> Royal Cathay
> (707) 451-2333

Remember, you must first have a wholesale license before you can order from these basket companies. Contact your state sales tax agency.

Holistic Housecleaning

Wanda Adelsberger has a successful Wisconsin-based part-time cleaning business with a twist—she only uses natural products when she cleans. No chemicals, just homemade products that are gentle on the environment. "It's the times. Anyone with any awareness of what is happening to our planet would consider using this kind of housecleaning service. I know people all over the country who are doing this and making it work." Wanda finds that it is a great way to make extra money to fund her daughter's interest in gymnastics.

Tools of the Trade

Instead of the chemical-laden commercial cleaning products available in grocery stores, Wanda's supplies are much simpler—a mixture of vinegar and water for surface cleaning, and baking soda for scrubbing. These two products form the basis for all of her cleaning. "Baking soda is a terrific substitute for abrasive scrubs like Comet. Wet the surface, shake it on, let it sit for ten minutes, and then clean it off. Works great—try it!" She also uses biodegradable Shaklee products, and feels that there are many high-quality, natural cleaning products available at health food stores. "Most people use too much stuff on their wood furniture; they just smother it with oils and waxes. Wood needs moisture; just a cloth barely dampened with water works fine to get the dust off and replenish the moisture content. That business of needing to wax and polish your furniture every week is just an old wives' tale."

Getting Started

One of the best features of offering a holistic housecleaning service is the speed with which you can get started. "I built this business up from no clients to seven clients within weeks," Wanda says. "The word of mouth just spreads like wildfire. A lot of people have just been waiting for something like this to come along."

To succeed in this as a part-time business, you must be confident of your skills and meticulous about details. "It is the little touches that are important—cleaning on top of fan blades, doing insides and tops of window ledges and blinds, dusting off light bulbs. Having someone else clean your house is a luxury, and in order to justify it that person must do a better job than the homeowner can do on his or her own. People will always apply stricter standards to a hired housecleaner's work than they would to their own, so be very thorough," Wanda recommends.

Setting Rates

Her prices are comparable to what other housecleaners are charging in her area. "Why charge more just because I use natural products? I want to encourage as many people as possible to live this way, not discourage them by making it costlier. It makes me angry that 'natural food' costs more than junk food; I don't want to make the same mistake in my own business."

Reading Labels

In Chicago, Heather's Holistic Housecleaning is also cleaning up on a part-time basis: $45 every time she cleans a medium-sized house. "This is an absolutely perfect way to make extra money," Heather proclaims. "And not only can you make extra money, but the work is so physical that I've lost a lot of weight, too!" Heather became a holistic housecleaner when she began reading the labels on cleaning products and noticing how many of them contained pollutants. Most abrasive scrubs, for instance, contain chlorine bleaching agents that create dioxin when they break down.

Before starting a cleaning service like Wanda's or Heather's, spend a bit of time reading the labels of standard cleaning products to acquaint yourself with the types of chemicals that you should avoid. Read environmental magazines like *Buzzworm, E,* or *Garbage* to develop a greater awareness of the issues. Your clients will expect you to have a fairly well developed knowledge of the subject.

Prop Rental

Do you live in a house filled with Victorian antiques? Mimi Luebbermann does, and not long ago she realized that her furniture and knickknacks could provide her with a terrific second income. A full-time writer, Mimi now has a SAM renting out her Victorian things to photographers needing props for the backgrounds of shots. To get started with prop rentals, she took color pictures of all of her Victorian things, put together a photo album, and began showing it to art directors at advertising agencies and to photographers. The standard rental fee for week-long use of a prop is from 10% to 20% of the replacement value, so a silver teaspoon that costs $20 to replace would rent for at least $2. An entire set of silverware worth $1,500 would rent for $150. Mimi specializes in supplying Victorian props for food photography, and reports a big demand for all types of silverware, interesting china platters and plates, lacy linens, and unusual serving pieces. Art Deco is also popular among food photographers. They don't need only Victorian or Art Deco props, of course; there is an abundant need for all kinds of things from all kinds of eras.

Mimi has real words of caution, however, about just how important it is to have pictures and documentation on everything that you rent out: "There are a few things out there that I don't think I will ever get back, simply because they were not well documented. It is very important to have a picture of every single piece that has been rented out, and for each of these pieces to be assigned a number. At any given time, then, I can just check my files and see that the Georgian silver serving spoon has not been returned and that it is time to bug the photographer! Develop a system to track your things, down to the teeniest item."

Seeing Your Old Props with a New Eye

After learning about Mimi's SAM, I started to look around at my own possesions with a different eye and realized that I had enough travel-related stuff from the 20s that I could easily put together a portfolio to show to photographers. Who wouldn't want one of my well-worn leather suitcases covered with vintage hotel stickers? And wouldn't my ostrich-skin jewlery box look fantastic in a high-gloss diamond advertisement? I also own a large collection of old travel postcards. What great background material for an ad! Mimi's success has inspired me to give this business a try, and if you have a great collection of things, you should try it too! Not everything will be of interest to photographers: I'm afraid that a collection of old gym socks won't quite cut it; but certainly a collection of old sports equipment would!

Having a broad-based assortment of things will increase the attractiveness of your collection to potential renters. Mimi recommends having at least 25 different items pictured in your promotional material. I was able to come up with the following 20s era collectibles to include in my "Classic Travel Era" prop offering:

several old leather suitcases (many with hotel and early plane stickers on the sides)

an ostrich-skin jewelry case

an original Chanel chantilly lace dress circa 1926

a large selection of old travel postcards

four antique oriental rugs

a polo trophy from a tournament in the south of France

assorted sterling silver pieces (including a classic 20s martini shaker)

many old family travel photos showing travelers in classic clothes posed in front of familiar monuments around the world

assorted tourist souvenirs from the era

a small Art Deco lamp

vintage train schedules and maps

antique cameras

old travel books

Rookwood pottery pieces

vintage U.S. passports

a dozen women's hats of all descriptions

The Business of Prop Rental

I spoke to advertising art director Brian Burch of the Burch Design Group about the business of prop rental: "We pass the cost of prop rental on to the client as part of the total cost of a project. The right props can sometimes make all the difference in a photo, turning an interesting photograph into a spectacular one. If I received a brochure from someone with a unique collection to rent out and I thought that I might use it someday, I would certainly file that information away. Approaching photographers directly is also a good method for people getting into the prop-rental business. You can buy lists of professional photographers from the professional organizations that they belong to, and you can also find them in stock workbooks. Anyone with a truly unique collection should be able to make prop renting work."

Tie-in Services

Mimi also recommends renting large pieces of furniture to realtors who need to furnish an empty high-priced house on the market. In the business this is called "house staging." Sometimes owners have to move to their new location before their old house sells, taking their furniture and leaving a stark empty house behind. Furnished houses sell faster, so realtors will rent furniture to create a better ambiance. One realtor has been known to actually ask the house-stagers to stay for the afternoon and bake cookies in the kitchen to create a warmer, more inviting atmosphere!

The Beauty of Renting

There is an old tale from the early days of the movie business that illustrates the beauty of renting something as a way of making money. One of the Warner brothers saw a film for the first time, noticed how many people had paid a nickel to watch it, and then marveled that afterward the theater owner still had the film and could show it over and over again. He decided right then and there to get into the movie business. What a great idea, to make money from something that you will still own later!

Personal Trainer

Chris Dominguez has been working in his spare time as a personal trainer for 12 years, making $30 an hour for his services. "If I lived in a larger metropolitan area like San Francisco or New York I could charge anywhere from $50 to $100, but in this small town I am happy with $30," he says. There is little overhead involved in becoming a personal trainer. Aside from business cards, education expenses, and certification fees, much of your hourly fee is profit.

Personal trainers design workouts for their clients, help them through the routine, and generally keep them on track with their fitness goals. "Since they pay me up front I give them a reason to show up at the gym! Who's going to blow off their workout if they know it means $30 down the drain?" Work as a personal trainer is a terrific way to go for aerobics instructors, athletes, dance students, or college students studying exercise physiology, nutrition, anatomy, or kinesiology. "If you are willing to go out and obtain the knowledge, then this is a great part-time business," Chris advises. The most in-demand times for working out with a personal trainer are early in the morning before work, or just after work. You could easily fit your clients in around a full-time or part-time job elsewhere. Personal trainers are popular with executives and professionals because they have limited time to exercise and can't afford to be injured.

Once you have the knowledge and expertise, it is a wise move to seek certification from the International Dance and Exercise Association, the American College of Sports Medicine, the National Strength and Conditioning Association, or the American Council on Exercise. The American Council on Sports Exercise in San Diego, California, does offer specialized training for budding personal trainers. Although personal fitness trainers do not have to be certified, it does help establish your credentials and validate your knowledge of the business.

Tie-in Services

Some personal trainers further supplement their incomes by providing space-planning consultation for in-home gyms. On a less complicated level, it is possible to advertise your services as a "workout partner" instead of a personal trainer. As a workout partner, you are merely there to exercise alongside your customer, inspiring him or her to keep going. Fees for workout partners would be far lower ($6 to $10 an hour), but you would be selling only your enthusiasm and inspiration, not your knowledge and skill in designing a training program.

Recycled Wood Products

In the 1920s, California winemakers built enormous fermentation vats from North Coast redwood in which to age their wine. Seventy years later, technology has changed to using stainless steel vats for that purpose. But what has become of all that beautiful old-growth redwood from the vats? Doug Chandler and Bert Weaverling have some of it, and they are happily making comfortable redwood rocking chairs up in the California foothills.

From Old Growth to New Growth

"I have a bad back," Doug told me, "and I designed the chair to fit me comfortably, with wide arms and a curved back. But it has turned out to be very popular with women who are either pregnant or nursing; the shape just seems to suit them." A full-time financial consultant to the state legislature, Doug, and his partner, retired woodworker Bert Weaverling, formed The Vintage Redwood Company as a part-time business they could both enjoy. "You just can't get wood like this anymore; loggers can't cut old-growth redwood any longer and nothing on the market is as well-seasoned as wood that has been holding wine for the last 70 years. The fact that this is recycled wood is a major selling point. It has beautiful color and depth. I like to think that each rocking chair we make contains a small part of California's lumber and wine-making history."

New Sources

Up in Oregon, an entrepreneurial couple is also using recycled wood in their unique bird feeders. Instead of using recycled redwood like The Vintage Redwood Company, they use mill ends, leftover pieces of lumber that would otherwise be thrown away or burned.

Sources for recycled wood are increasing. There are secondhand wood dealers, demolitions, old barns, and old wood lots to comb for usable material. To recondition wood you must have the proper equipment—a table saw and a small planer. Reconditioning recycled wood is a relatively simple process, and both you and your customers will be contributing to the health of the earth.

Outlets for selling products made from recycled wood are also increasing: stores like The Nature Company, the Sierra Club Bookstore, and countless other small environmentally friendly or outdoor-theme stores are terrific. Uniqueness really sells in this handicraft category. The Vintage Redwood Company does not advertise, has no glossy brochure, yet consistently sells chairs for upwards of $300 just by word of mouth!

Special Occasion Sign Rentals

Birthdays, anniversaries, weddings, job promotions, births, and all manner of noteworthy occasions can be celebrated in high style with a "special occasion sign" planted on the recipient's front lawn. Part-time entrepreneur Dean Handy rents his Yard Cards to folks who want a high-profile celebration. "With the birth announcements, it is usually the dad who orders the sign. Fortieth birthdays and the like, it is bound to be either the wife or a couple of friends playing a trick." Dean has an inventory of 30 signs for various occasions, and each one rents for $25 a day, $35 for three days, or $50 for a whole week. The cost includes delivery, installation, and pickup, as well as the painting of a personalized message onto the sign. The big wooden signs are all handmade by Dean, based on drawings that an artist does for him. He blows up the design and traces it onto the wood and then paints it in himself. Big bunny rabbits for birthdays and birth announcements, a large "Grim Reaper" that is popular for 30th and 40th birthdays, teddy bears, giraffes, and a carousel horse are among the signs that Dean rents out. Although Dean is an independent operator who created his business from scratch, there is a nationwide sign-rental franchise company that specializes in large storks for birth announcements, so he stays away from storks.

The special occasion sign business is well suited for weekend entrepreneurs. "Most rentals do take place on the weekends," Dean told me. "People like to have the signs out front during birthday parties, and that is generally when they are held."

Getting Started

When first starting out, Dean was able to generate business right away because he worked on his signs on his own front lawn and attracted a lot of attention from passersby. He also plants the signs in his own front yard on occasion, but recommends against overdoing it in order to avoid annoying your neighbors. He has tried several different methods of marketing—advertising, placing flyers in card stores, and even setting up displays at bridal fairs. Business has its ups and downs, but he averages about 20 sign rentals a month.

Dean has some good advice for weekend entrepreneurs who think that their area could support this type of business—

plan carefully! "Draw up a business plan that takes all aspects of the business into consideration, everything from financing to marketing. Once you draw up your plan, stick with it! If you don't have a business plan or outline you will stray from your original intentions very quickly. Even though this is a part-time business, take it seriously and make sure that you allot enough of your time and energy to it."

Teaching Special Classes

Do you have a skill, hobby, or talent that others would really like to learn? A great way to make weekend money is to teach private classes to small groups of people. Successful small classes can be held on a variety of topics—creative writing, foreign languages, literary and historical topics, cooking, woodworking, crafts, even etiquette! Many years ago, I taught a class on self-publishing to a group of ten people who had each paid $45 for an afternoon. I rented a room in a community center for $30 and the remaining $420 was profit! The only reason I have not continued to teach is that I do not enjoy standing in front of a room full of strangers. If you are shy, this is not a SAM for you. But for those who are bold enough, teaching can be a very rewarding experience, both emotionally and financially. "Our society is going through an exciting explosion in lifelong learning. More people than ever are becoming involved in classes and educational events, for personal reasons and for professional reasons," says William Draves, founder and Director of the Learning Resources Network.

Novelist and screenwriter *(Inside Moves)* Todd Walton teaches a six-week course in creative writing to groups of eight for the modest sum of $122. Classes are held in his living room every Wednesday night. He provides soft pillows and all the Chinese tea you can drink. Students bring their own paper and pens. His classes are so popular that he no longer has to advertise: the word of mouth is so tremendous that a long waiting list exists for months in advance.

Bart Brodsky, the founder of Open Exchange in Berkeley, California, says that the opportunities for teachers and topics are endless. "The YMCAs, exercise salons, dance studios, New Age meditation retreats, and special interest clubs are all vying for a piece of the educational pie. The range and the functions of the activities—intellectual, social, ethical, and spiritual—are beyond the scope of any one, one thousand, or ten thousand providers to handle." So find your teaching niche and get going!

The ABCs of Teaching

Few things could be as simple as teaching a class. Once you have determined that you have knowledge that other folks would pay to learn (or you go out and learn something specifically so that you can make extra money teaching it to others), you must follow a few short simple steps:

1. Find a location in which to hold the class. Your own home would be the least expensive, of course, but it might not be the most desirable. Take a good, hard look at your surroundings and try to see them from the standpoint of a complete stranger who has arrived to take a class. Would you be delighted at the location, or dismayed? If you do not honestly think that strangers would be delighted to spend several hours in your living room, then you must rent a location. Churches and schools are good places to look. They often have community rooms that can be rented for a short period of time for a modest sum. Make sure that the price of the room includes the use of the chairs! A blackboard on the wall or an overhead projector might also be needed, depending on your teaching methods.

2. Advertise for students. Small community newspapers are ideal for this, as are the free bulletin boards in bookstores, community centers, or wherever else your potential students might go. Many communities have organized learning programs like the Learning Annex in New York and San Francisco, and Open Exchange in Berkeley. These programs are always on the lookout for new and interesting courses to offer and are always open to hearing new ideas about classes. They will take a large percentage of your class fee, but it is a great way to get started.

3. Plan your curriculum. Make sure that you have enough to talk about for the entire class. It takes a lot of talking to fill up two or three hours. Plan your class in such a way that there are many points at which you can stop and open it up for students' questions. Students expect learning in this type of class to be quick, informative, and fun. Prepare handouts and other materials that your students can examine during class and take home afterward. Prepare exercises that the whole class can do. Todd Walton's creative writing class consists primarily of short exercises that he has developed to spur creativity in his own work. The students do the exercises in the quiet of his own living room, breaking afterward to read their work aloud.

4. Try to anticipate problems that might occur and be prepared to deal with them. Make sure you have a backup plan in case something goes wrong with your scheduled location or for some reason you need to reschedule the date and time of your class.

5. Teach! With each class you teach you will learn something new, enabling you to refine and improve your class continuously. You may find that you can soon teach a more advanced level of the same class, which will give you an opportunity to work with the same students all over again. If you did a good job with the beginner-level class they will be happy to learn from you once more. It is useful to hand out an anonymous evaluation form at the end of your class so that you will instantly have feedback on your students' reactions, good or bad. This will help you spot problems right away and take steps to improve for the next group.

Setting Rates

Prices for classes vary widely. To determine your price you should consider the following: How well do I know my subject? How professional are my teaching skills? How difficult is it to obtain this knowledge? Always start with a modest price for your first few classes; $25 for an afternoon class would be acceptable. Another way to get started is to offer a "free introductory class" as a way to get potential students interested. Having started modestly, once you become more comfortable with your topic and start to see positive feedback from your students, you may be justified in raising your price. Before you commit to a particular price, do check out the competition to see if similar classes are being offered and at what rate. Take your expenses and costs into consideration as well.

Educating Yourself

A good basic book to read on this subject is:

> *The Teaching Marketplace: Make Money with Freelance Teaching, Corporate Trainings, and on the Lecture Circuit*
> Bart Brodsky and Janet Geis
> Community Resource Institute Press
> (510) 525-9663
> $14.95

Thinking It Through

For most of the business ideas detailed here you must possess one important element—creativity. There are no books, no business plans that can really tell you how to make them succeed. Large doses of passion, creativity, and imagination will come in handy. If you do not think that you could succeed in a business that you will, to a great extent, be creating on your own, then these are not the ideas for you. Better to stick to more staid, tried-and-true businesses like those found in "Back to Basics" or "Old-Fashioned Money."

Finding Comfort in the Spotlight

Publicity is another key element in the success of these businesses, and you must also ask yourself if you really want publicity. Not everyone feels comfortable talking to the press, giving radio interviews, or standing in front of television cameras. The press would love to write a story about someone with a holistic housecleaning business, or someone who gives tours of the local graveyard, and if you thrive on attention then you really do have what it takes. If you are not comfortable in the spotlight, one possibility would to be to take on a partner in some of these businesses. Perhaps your spouse or one of your children would better handle the publicity and promotion.

To learn more about how to get free publicity for yourself or your business, you might take a look at:

> *Publicity Kit: A Complete Guide for Entrepreneurs, Small*
> *Businesses, and Nonprofit Organizations*
> Jeanette Smith
> John Wiley and Sons
> $14.95

Take a chance on some of these oddball ideas. Some of the most successful people in the world are businesspeople who managed to make a quirky business idea work in a big way. And remember one of life's old rules: the biggest rewards lie at the end of the biggest risks!

Chapter Seven

Available Talent— Opportunities for Artists and Musicians

For those of you lucky enough to be gifted with either artistic or musical talent, there are many creative SAMS out there for hardworking weekend entrepreneurs. If you work all week long in a straight-laced business environment, all decked out in suit and tie, why not break loose on the weekends and indulge your creative pursuits for extra cash? What a terrific way to balance all of your needs and talents!

Art Parties—One-Night-Only Galleries

During the summer I received a beautiful invitation to a garden party. Knowing what a lovely home and backyard my friend had, I eagerly made plans to attend. Once I walked into the garden on the afternoon of the party, however, I began to notice something unusual—scattered around the gravel walkway were small tables filled with interesting pieces of art for sale. My friend Julia was throwing an art party!

131

"I was having coffee with several of my friends from the art college," she told me later, "and we were bemoaning the fact that it is so hard to make any money as an artist. It is hard to get a gallery to represent you, and even if you are represented you will probably get to have a showing of your art only every other year or so. The rest of the time your work just gathers dust in the back room of the gallery. So we had a group brainstorm: why not have our own Saturday afternoon show and sale combined with a summer garden party? Each of us would have a section of the garden in which we could build our own display area. We would all pitch in together to combine names for the mailing list. We also shared expenses for the food, drinks, and printing and mailing invitations."

A Magical Setting

It was a magical setting. Among the daisy beds there was a display of African sculpture; large oil paintings were hung against the whitewashed fence. Inside the house Julia displayed her ceramic sculptures of shoes and purses, each piece artfully nestled in draped cloth. I promptly spent $60 on one of Julia's sculptures and $20 on a set of ceramic mugs made by another local artist. And I noticed that I was by no means the only one buying art; many of the guests wandered the paths clutching newly purchased pieces. In addition to having bought some wonderful art, I experienced a fine afternoon party, with lots of music, tasty food, and interesting guests. "It was simple to plan, enjoyable to attend, and we all ended up selling a great deal of art. We think it will be an annual event," Julia told me afterward. And I think I will be there for the next one, too!

One Night Only

Another version of the art party is a "one-night-only" gallery. Where an art party is a casual outdoors affair, a one-night-only gallery has more of an "event" feel to it and is a larger undertaking.

To stage a one-night-only gallery you must first find a suitable empty gallery space. A successful Sacramento art promoter borrows friends' large apartments for his one-night events. Large rooms with plain white walls work the best. It is important to remove any art already on the walls and push excess furniture into a spare room to create a suitable gallery feel and make room for guests. A terrific time to approach someone about using their house or apartment is just before they move out: the furniture will already be gone and the owner will not be inconvenienced.

Finding Customers

Postcards are a good, inexpensive way to alert art lovers to your event. Mail them not only to your friends and supporters but to any lists of potential collectors and art lovers that you can obtain—perhaps members of the local museum or patrons of other galleries. Send press releases about your one-night-only gallery to local newspapers and ask them to list it on the events page. This is a free service in most newspapers and, if they are intrigued by your event, they might just send a reporter to cover it!

Calligraphy

Calligraphy is the art of beautiful handwriting, something that few of us possess. Over the centuries a highly stylized version of calligraphy has developed and those who already have mastered it or can develop the talent will find that they have a highly marketable skill.

Wedding Invitations

The biggest demand for custom calligraphers is in hand addressing wedding invitations or other event announcements. Hand addressing wedding invitations is very exacting, so once you determine how many envelopes you can address in an hour you should set your rates so that you make at least $30 an hour. For instance, if you discover that you can address 50 cards an hour, then you should charge $60 to address 100 wedding invitations. Not too shabby for two hours' work! You must be very careful when addressing wedding invitations, though; because most people print about as many as they plan to send out, you will have a very small margin for error.

Special Recognitions

Besides invitations, another need for beautifully hand-lettered work can be found in awards, proclamations, and special recognitions. Many corporations and community organizations hand out special awards to employees and members who deserve special recognition. The awards are that much more meaningful when the recipient's name and achievement are recorded in graceful calligraphy. You should have a simple fee structure to cover these assignments—$25 per award would be reasonable.

Finding Clients

A good way to get word of your skills out to businesses and organizations is to send beautifully lettered notes to the public affairs and public relations offices of large companies. Calligraphers can also alert local invitation printers that their services are for hire. Friendly printers may even let you leave a brochure or flyer about your services on their counter.

Clowns, Puppet Shows, and Magicians

Clowning Around

Are you always the center of attention at family gatherings? Famous for your silly act at office parties? Maybe you should take up clowning as a part-time profession! Pansy Potts did, in a career move that she calls "serendipity." Clowns are in great demand on weekends at children's parties, Christmas shows, and company picnics. Everybody loves a clown, and if you really love children (you shouldn't try this if you don't) you will also love the $80 an hour that clowns command for their performances!

Pansy worked at many things before becoming a weekend clown, but nothing else was as satisfying. She encourages women in particular to take up clowning: "Clowns can be kind of scary to young children, and women clowns are smaller and not so intimidating." In addition to her clown act, she tells stories, makes balloon animals, and stages a puppet show.

Clown College

And where did she learn to do all of this? Clown College! For the serious student of clowning, La Crosse University in La Crosse, Wisconsin, offers clown classes in the summer. The teachers are the very same clowning instructors that teach at Ringling Brothers Clown College in Florida. Once clowns learn the basics, they can stay ahead of the competition and keep their skills sharp by joining Clowns International to continue their training and learning.

Getting Started

Although becoming a "community clown" (instead of a circus clown) can be both financially and emotionally rewarding, Pansy warns that start-up costs can be high. Investing in an outfit and professional makeup is expensive, as is advertising for clients. "It doesn't happen all at once," Pansy says. "It might take six months before you actually start to see some money. Polish your skills in the meantime by performing for free at local convalescent homes and hospitals."

Educating Yourself

To learn more about becoming a clown and the opportunities available for weekend clowning, you might subscribe to the following magazine:

> *Calliope*
> Clowns of America
> P.O. Box 570
> Lake Jackson, Texas 77566-0570

Wavy Gravy, a longtime 60s proponent of clowning around, teaches special one-week sessions for adults who want to learn the fine art of clowning. For information contact him at:

> Camp Winnarainbow
> Circus and Performing Arts Camp
> 1301 Henry Street
> Berkeley, California 94709
> (510) 525-4304

Puppets

"Puppetry is an art form," Mary Charles told me, "and if properly learned it can also become a very lucrative one." Mary's part-time puppet company, Puppets Unlimited, runs a thriving birthday party business in Hawaii. In addition to birthday parties, she suggests incorporating educational materials such as local legends and myths into your puppet shows as a way to enter into the school-visit market. At an average of $100 for an afternoon show, puppet shows can provide a tidy source of extra money.

Educating Yourself

To learn puppetry, Mary suggests that you first attend as many shows as you can to get a sense of what other local puppeteers are doing. National puppetry conventions are held annually that include workshops and seminars on puppet making, script writing, and performance techniques. Contact the Puppeteers of America for more information. They also publish the *Puppetry Journal,* which will help keep you informed of goings-on in the puppetry community.

Magicians

"I first learned magic when I was a kid. I was on crutches for several years, and so instead of playing sports I taught myself to perform magic tricks," Bill Devon told me. A full-time parking enforcement officer, Bill gets a lot of kicks and a steady source of extra income by working as a magician. "For most private birthday parties I charge $75 per show, but for a larger business or organization my rate is more like $150. On average, I do about four shows a month." Besides birthday parties, he does shows at fairs, on cruises, at reunions and community events. After many years in the magic business, referrals are the major source of his jobs, but he also runs small ads in community papers.

Getting Started

How do you become a paid magician? Bill learned from books and by exchanging ideas with other magicians. "Other magicians will help you out; it is a friendly fraternity of sorts," he says. To find other magicians in your area, check out your local magic store. They should be able to put you in contact with the local chapter of the IBM, the International Brotherhood of Magicians. Then pull out that old pack of playing cards and start practicing!

Custom Murals and Children's Furniture

"I majored in art in college," Sandy Hoover told me, "but I never really did anything with it. I went to work as a landscaper and did that for several years. Then my sister asked me to paint a mural on the wall in her new baby's room, and I enjoyed it so much that I decided to get back into art."

Wall Antics

Sandy's business, Wall Antics, specializes in small or large custom murals for children's rooms. Each mural takes several weeks to complete, working primarily on the weekends when the homeowner is around. "I am bonded with personal liability," Sandy says, "in case I spill paint all over their carpet or something. I really recommend covering yourself that way! Don't take chances."

She paints one or two murals a month, charging anywhere from $500 to $1,500, depending on the size and the complexity of the design. Many of her jobs have come via word of mouth, but she also tries to work with local interior decorators for referrals, and has on occasion advertised in small newsletters catering to parents of small children.

adrawables

Connecticut-based artist Elizabeth Katz also advertises her mural painting company, adrawables, in small parenting magazines. A full-time mother, she sets aside two days a week to market her murals to schools, showcase homes, and hospitals. "I let schools know that I am available to paint murals in the library, gym, cafeteria, or wherever else the walls need to be livened up!"

Elizabeth majored in art history in college and spent several years working in publishing before the birth of her son, Ben. She hasn't yet painted a mural in his room, but has given him another of her products—a custom-painted bureau. "I do more furniture than murals right now," she explained, "rocking chairs, toy chests, stools, and small table and chair sets. No one has asked to have a bed painted, though. Most parents want the furniture painted to match the wallpaper or the curtains."

Painted children's furniture and custom room murals are growing in popularity as the Baby Boomers become parents themselves. Creating a weekend pursuit that caters to this trend will assure extra income for years to come. Elizabeth recommends placing samples of your painted furniture in children's clothing stores to attract potential customers.

Face Painting

Cheeks painted with rainbows, clouds, and stars were standard fare at 60s love-ins and rock concerts, falling from popularity for a decade or two. But, like platform shoes and bell-bottom jeans, they're back. . . . Take a look at the faces of small children at any large public attraction like a county fair or an amusement park, and you will see tiny Mutant Ninja Turtles, happy faces (they're back too!), and rainbows painted on almost every one. An artist with painting skills can easily find weekend work as a freelance face painter to meet the demands of these young art patrons.

"Most kids ask for whatever cartoon character happens to be popular, Disney or movie characters like Batman," explains Cathleen Swanson. "I encourage them to want things from nature like fish, insects, or flowers. A very popular trick is to paint their entire face to look like a lion or a cat. They love it." A substitute teacher during the week, Cathleen works only one or two days a month as a face painter. Summer months are the most active as there are more events held then.

Setting Rates

"I make $100 an afternoon," says Cathleen, "depending on what kind of event it is. If it is a charity event I might charge less, but if it is a big crafts fair or other for-profit affair, then I do ask for $100." Event organizers pay for the face painter's services so that children can line up and have their faces decorated for free. "Parents love it, and it makes the children feel very special," Cathleen says.

Finding Clients

In addition to outdoor attractions like fairs and concerts, events sponsored by city parks and recreation departments may desire the services of face painters. Organizers of birthday parties and company picnics also like to have face painters around for the kids. Cathleen finds work by contacting the public relations departments at hospitals to let them know she is available on Saturdays and Sundays to paint faces at parties and community "wellness" fairs, and she pays close attention to advertisements about big events. She makes it a point to call the organizers to inquire about hiring. "Radio stations are also a prime source for work," she says. "They run many outdoor promotions and events that use face painters as part of the entertainment."

Tools of the Trade

Supplies are few, just several brushes and a good selection of colors. Cathleen uses a brand of water-based theatrical paint from Germany, Kryolon, available at costume and theatrical stores and sometimes also found in art supply or hobby stores.

Tie-in Services

Although face painting does seem most popular among small children, a new trend is catching on among adults that could be an additional service a talented face painter could offer—temporary tattoos. More detailed and time-consuming work, but it is another great way to make money! Using the same water-based theatrical paint but with smaller, finer brushes, a talented painter could charge up to $25 per tattoo. Not a bad way to make extra money on a sunny afternoon.

House Portraits and Custom Stationery

I grew up on a street lined with old family homes on one side and a vast green park on the other. It was a terrific place for a kid to roam, and it was also fertile ground for enterprising artists with architectural-rendering skills. Once every two or three years the doorbell would ring and a smiling artist would suggest that my folks engage his or her services to sketch, paint, or photograph our house. The prices ranged from $150 for a photograph (my parents declined) to $85 for a pen-and-ink sketch (my parents agreed). The woman who successfully sold her artistic talent came prepared with a sample book of portraits that she had done in other towns and neighborhoods. After shaking hands on the deal, she agreed to return the following day to render the portrait.

For several hours she sat perched on a stool at the side of the driveway as she carefully studied each element of the house and translated it as simply and elegantly as she could onto her sketch pad. At the end of the afternoon, she rang the doorbell again and proudly presented my parents with her work, an eight-by-ten-inch pen-and-ink drawing of their house, trees and all.

While accepting the check for her efforts, she suggested that in addition to framing and displaying the drawing, they might want to take it to a printer and have custom stationery made from it. An excellent idea, they agreed; and for the last few years, whenever I am in trouble I have received terse notes from my mother on custom-folded note cards imprinted on the front with the portrait of their house. It tends to soften the blow. . . .

Getting Started

Wealthy neighborhoods are prime areas in which to sell house portraits, but more modest areas might also be good areas to scout. To get started you should first do several portraits of either friends' homes or the homes of complete strangers (who knows, perhaps you can sell one to them once you get established!), making certain that you try several different architectural styles in order to display your range. Assemble samples of your work in a handsome and expensive-looking photo album; print some business cards; decide on your prices; dress professionally for your initial contacts, and start pounding the pavement. Make certain that your price is within reason; don't price yourself too high or you will never get this business off the ground.

In addition to painting or drawing a straight portrait, you might also suggest that you could produce a snowy winter setting for the portrait so that it could be used for custom Christmas cards. This is certain to appeal to well-heeled homeowners hoping to impress their friends on the holidays! Charge a bit more to "winterize" the scene.

Printmakers and silk-screen artists can also sell custom stationery based on houses. The project would take more time than a three-hour sketch, but the product would be just as appealing. With this type of product you would be agreeing to deliver designed and printed cards or stationery instead of just a simple portrait. Consider your prices carefully; you must find a price for 200 or more custom-designed and printed cards that will be both affordable for a customer and profitable for you. I spoke to an enterprising art student who warned that this is "labor-intensive," but ultimately worth the effort.

Tie-in Services

Custom house portraits are also of interest to real estate agents looking for an inexpensive way to spruce up a marketing brochure for a particular property. A small drawing or sketch of the house for sale is not only a classy touch but less expensive to print than a photo. Once you become an experienced house portrait artist, you might consider making your own flyer or brochure and dropping it off at realtors' offices to attract more work. What better way to spend a weekend than selling a portrait or two?

Pet Portraits

If your artistic talent does not lend itself to house portraits, consider animal portraits. Many pet owners are devoted to their animals both in life and in death, and are willing to pay large sums of money to have their beloved pet immortalized on canvas. This work is best done from a photograph, as the animals themselves are seldom cooperative about sitting still.

Mobile Art Gallery

Artist Kathy Lee had an idea—why not bring her artwork right to people's homes and offices so that they could make their selections knowing what looked good hanging on the walls? And why not take the work of other artists along with her while she made her rounds? With that idea a new part-time business was born, a mobile art gallery.

"I'm a potter, but other than my own stuff I am willing to sell only works on paper. Paintings and prints are relatively easy to transport; pottery and sculpture are not! I wanted to design the whole business to fit in the back seat of my car, and so that was what I focused on. Besides my own art, I represent the work of 20 other artists." Rather than take 50% or more of the selling price like a standard gallery, Kathy keeps 40% of the proceeds from the other artists' work. The artists are pleased to get a greater percentage, and also pleased at Kathy's gung-ho attitude toward finding new clients for their art. Most artists are much more creative than business-minded. Talented people with the organizational skills to pull this off are a real treasure and will find it easy to interest artists in representation.

Finding Clients

Kathy's first step in starting up was to join the local Chamber of Commerce in order to be able to attend the "business mixer" functions offered to members. "I met a lot of clients that way. I would put on my most businesslike outfit and chat up the executives. Eventually the conversation would get around to what I did, and in many cases I walked away with an appointment to come to their office or home and show the art. Art in an office projects an air of sophistication; but to tell you the truth, most of the businesspeople that I've talked to were pretty intimidated by the thought of going into a gallery to make a purchase. It can be kind of scary. Once they realized that I would bring the art to them, they were really relieved. It is easy for people to make up their minds if you are standing right in their living room or office with the piece hanging on the wall. It looks good, they can afford it, so why not buy?" In addition to her activities with the Chamber of Commerce, Kathy has also advertised in local business newspapers and publications, and receives many referrals from satisfied clients.

Setting Rates

Start-up costs are modest for a business like this. In addition to joining the Chamber, Kathy had business cards made. "The Chamber membership was expensive," she warns, "but it really did pay off." Another advantage to a mobile art gallery is that there really is no overhead. You are not paying rent on a fancy retail space hoping that art-buying customers will wander in by chance. You can simply store the art and crafts in an extra bedroom or closet until it is time for the next appointment.

Most of the art that Kathy has for sale is priced in the $200 to $400 range, but she does handle more expensive pieces. Offering layaway terms to her clients is another bonus, although she does not deliver the piece until the account is fully settled.

Making It Work

A mobile art gallery is a perfect SAM for a working artist. You determine your own selling hours, and are completely free to work on your art whenever you want. Most of your clients will want you to come in the evening, or late in the afternoon for office appointments (make sure that you find out in advance how many decision-makers there are in the home or office, and that all of them will be available!). Once you begin to set original prints and paintings out that catch their eye, you are on your way to a sale! "I recommend it," says Kathy Lee. "It works for me."

Thinking It Through

Before you turn your talents into a business, you must first ask yourself the same sorts of questions that I recommended that crafters ask themselves—can you handle rejection? Not everyone will wholeheartedly embrace your artistic or musical style; taste is not universal. How will you feel if a potential customer takes one look at the samples of custom house portraits that you have put together so carefully and says, "Gee, you want me to pay money for that? Get real!" You must learn not to take these rejections personally; it is all in a day's work and many an acclaimed artist has had their work ridiculed.

Your artwork might also be a private pleasure that you won't enjoy selling. Some artists truly feel that they are "prostituting" their talent by trying to pander to a broad audience. Decide whether you will feel comfortable showing your work to the world.

Be businesslike in your endeavors. Artists have an undeserved reputation for being flaky and unreliable, so do all that you can to allay this impression. Dress professionally when necessary and always behave like a businessperson when dealing with your clients.

Keep trying, and you just might find that your God-given talent is also a godsend when it comes to making extra money!

Chapter Eight

Cooking Up Dollars— Making Money in the Kitchen

When the weekend rolls around, we all like to indulge a bit. What better way to make extra money than to cater to that universal craving for tasty food? Specialty foods, baked goods, gourmet fruit stands, and many other food-related businesses are solid ways for weekend entrepreneurs to develop SAMs by cashing in on this need.

Baking to Order

Maia Amos has been baking for years. She baked her own daughter's wedding cake and has made countless cakes for friends and relatives and community fund-raisers. And so, after years of giving her talent away, she decided to do it for money! Her business, Mother of the Groom, specializes in baking the "groom's cake," the extra cake that is traditionally given in small pieces to guests at the end of the reception. "The single girls are supposed to take these small pieces of cake and put them under their pillows, and then they will dream of their future mates. It's a very old tradition, but not many caterers and wedding cake shops offer a groom's cake.

Maia is a retired computer programmer who divides her time between baking and volunteering in the local Sierra Club gift store. "Compared to computers, baking cakes is a whole lot more fun! Right now I am operating on a pretty small scale, renting space from a friend with a professional kitchen when I have an order to fill. If I didn't have a cat, I would remodel my kitchen into a certified professional space; you can't ever have animals around a professional kitchen. I don't suppose you'd like a cat?" she joked during our interview.

Groom's Cake

Maia has put together a picture portfolio of finished cakes to show to potential customers and she works at several dessert-tasting fundraisers and bridal fairs giving away samples of the ornately frosted dark fruit cake that is traditionally used for a groom's cake. Her prices vary according to size; a groom's cake that will serve 60 people would run about $100.

Tie-in Services

In addition to her groom's cakes, Maia has also advertised her availability to do customized holiday baking. "Few people have the time to do up their Christmas breads and cookies," she says, "so I step in and bake up whatever they have in mind. That way they can impress their friends with little gift bags of home-baked goodies without the time and effort in the kitchen. Of course, they never confess that they haven't baked it them-selves, so I'm afraid that I don't get any word-of-mouth advertising on this!"

Custom Cooking

"I've been making an extra $150 a week for the past ten years," says Eleanor Nathan in New York. "After all this time, my clients say they just don't know what they'd do without me!" Eleanor does what she calls "custom home cooking" for a professional couple, both busy doctors who have neither the time nor the skill to cook meals at home but still enjoy having home-cooked meals. Eleanor cooks meals for this busy couple in her own kitchen. The meals are prepared according to the couple's personal taste and health requirements—only fish and chicken, light on the spices. Eleanor then brings two meals on Monday and two on Wednesday, and says that she has become "an expert on what freezes well!" Her rates are $28 per meal for two, not including the cost of the groceries. And as for training, although Eleanor happens to be a graduate of the Cordon Bleu in Paris and has restaurant and catering experience, she believes that what busy couples crave is not fancy food, but just good basic meals that any good home cook can prepare.

Finding Clients

"I cook only for this one couple, sometimes while working full-time at other things. If I had more time and energy I would add more clients. There is a real need for this kind of service in a big city; if you are in the right area you can really do well," Eleanor asserts. Her advice to new custom cooks looking for clients is to advertise their services at senior citizen condos where well-heeled retired people might enjoy having specially cooked meals delivered to them. Hospitals and large office buildings are also filled with on-the-go potential customers looking for good food but lacking the time to cook it themselves. Few people can afford to have a live-in cook or chef, but who wouldn't enjoy a reasonably priced home-cooked meal delivered on a regular basis?

Unique Dining

Tom Manning and Nadine Gold's business, Unique Dining, serves many clients. Both are full-time professional chefs in Orange County, California, who started their own side business in the fall of 1992. For the reasonable price of $260, Tom and

Nadine will customize a menu to suit the client's tastes, do all of the grocery shopping, arrive at the client's home and, using the client's kitchen, prepare enough food to last two work-weeks. They will then wrap the meals and mark them clearly, freeze them, and leave the kitchen spotless! Although $260 sounds high, clients are getting ten meals for two people; that breaks down to $13 per person per meal, less than the price of dinner in a modest restaurant.

To find out how to start a business like Tom and Nadine's you can call the United States Personal Chef Association at (800) 547-7915. They offer a complete business training system.

Meals by the Calendar

On a much larger scale than Eleanor's individualized cooking or Unique Dining's in-home service are home-cooked meal delivery services that advertise to the general public and that may be used on a one-time-only basis. Home on the Range and Homemade Express are two businesses in California's East Bay Area that mail out a calendar with a month's worth of meals listed. If customers call to place their order by 2:30 in the afternoon, they can arrive home from work that evening and find a delicious meal waiting on their front porch. Succeeding in a business of this scale is much more difficult, much more costly to undertake, and would require a partner or job-sharing arrangement for moms at home. A professional kitchen would also be required for a business of this size.

Coffee Delivery Service

I was researching weekend entrepreneurs in the state of Washington when I discovered Sarah Buck's business card in an Anacortes bookstore. As a devout coffee lover myself, I could immediately see the need for her enterprise, "Kaffee Klatsch," a gourmet coffee company which offers home delivery of fresh roasted and specially blended coffees. "My husband is in the military," she explained to me, "so I needed to develop a business that could move across the country if necessary, and that was not tied down by having a storefront." Employed full-time in the field of human resources when she founded Kaffee Klatsch, Sarah is now pursuing only her coffee business. Motivated by a real love for fresh roasted coffee, she researched suppliers until she found a solid wholesale contact in San Francisco which offered a superior product for a terrific price. She buys in bulk from her supplier and then repackages the whole beans in smaller quantities for her customers, charging a 100% markup to ensure a tidy profit. "I offer not only convenience for my clients but a great product at a great price. Here in Washington, coffee drinkers have become accustomed to the dark, heavy roasted beans that the Seattle roasters sell. I have educated many of my clients to an appreciation of the lighter, more delicate roasts."

Finding Customers

It is very possible to run a coffee delivery service on a part-time basis, Sarah believes, depending on how many customers you plan to have. In her early days she went door-to-door giving out small samples in order to attract customers and also spread the word about her service among family and friends. At that time, she offered her coffee delivery service to residential neighborhoods, delivering on her bicycle; but she soon realized that servicing businesses would be another area for potential profits. She now has several business customers who order ten pounds a week. In designing her business, she followed the model of the old-fashioned neighborhood milkman, establishing weekly or biweekly deliveries to regular customers. The customers pay Sarah by leaving a check in the mailbox or under the mat.

During the holidays she offers additional products for her customers in a "Best of the Pacific Northwest" gift basket containing smoked salmon, local jams, and of course, coffee. Despite the popularity of these items, Sarah does not plan to stray from her roots. "I believe that in order to succeed in any business you must have a real love and passion for your product. Many people have gone into the coffee business because it is popular, not because they love it. I am motivated by a passion for good coffee, and that is what I want to sell." Sarah shares this passion and knowledge with her customers by also holding coffee-tasting parties to let them try other types of beans and roasts. Delicious, timely, and rewarding, the home coffee delivery can really brew success for a weekend entrepreneur!

Coffee Bean Stand

Another coffee-related weekend SAM is to sell fresh roasted beans by the pound at farmers' markets. "I've been doing this on the weekend for eight years now," Diane Howe said. "I buy the beans from four different roasters here in town so that I can offer my customers a broad selection." Weekends at the farmers' market in Roseville, California, are always busy; it is one of the largest and most established in the state, and Diane's booth does not come cheap.

Coffee and Collectibles

Diane bought her business, Coffee and Collectibles, from a friend. "She was carrying only 10 types of coffee beans; I now offer my customers over 70 varieties. I also sell coffee filters and small coffee grinders. I've thought about carrying espresso machines or coffee makers, but I think that the price of most equipment is too high for the casual weekend customer stopping by to pick up a pound of beans." A stay-at-home mom during the week, Diane has evolved her business into a simple routine. "Monday morning I phone in orders for more product, the shipment arrives on Thursday, and then I work throughout the day on Saturday and Sunday. What could be simpler?"

Tips for Success

Diane has important advice to offer any weekend entrepreneur—take the long view of success. "I see some stand operators counting their till every hour and deciding whether or not they are a success based on what they made that day. You can't approach it like that if you really aim to succeed; you have to look at a year's worth of proceeds to decide what the true picture is."

She also recommends against starting a "copy cat" business at a farmers' market, "Your product must be original and of very high quality if you hope to succeed. If you burn a customer with shoddy product once, that's it. They will never forget. I've seen lots of people fail here over the last eight years, and it was because they were trying to fool the public with their product. That never works."

When working a stand at a farmers' market, Diane warns that operators need to pay attention at all times. "Some people just wander away from their stand in the middle of the day! You have to enjoy people if you want to make this work, because you have to be cheerful and attentive all the time. In the summer it gets hot, in the winter it gets cold, but you have to stand there and smile anyway."

Coffee Roasters

Although Diane does not roast the beans herself, there are successful coffee roasters plying their trade at farmer's markets. Coffee roaster Chris Trujillo realized years ago that, while spending the work week as a coffee roaster for a commercial company, he could set up shop with a small electric roaster at outdoor events on the weekend and bring in extra money. "The smell of roasting beans always brings a great crowd," he

'and many of those who come to watch end up leav-
pound or two."

Educating Yourself

Like wine, coffee is a connoisseur item with many complex
elements, and in order to sell it effectively you should develop
a true appreciation for it. The Specialty Coffee Association of
America has educational material available to help businesspeople learn about all aspects of the coffee business. They also
sponsor an annual conference at which many informative seminars are held that can help you learn more about the coffee
business. Here's how you can reach them:

> Specialty Coffee Association of America
> One World Trade Center, Suite 800
> Long Beach, California 90831
> (310) 983-8090

Espresso Carts

How many coffee-related SAMs can there be? More than you
think! All across the country, coffee drinkers are reaching for
something other than stale canned coffee grounds. Fresh
roasted and ground coffee is a new national passion. And coffee drinkers don't want a good cup of coffee only at home, the
office, or in a restaurant; they want it everywhere! Espresso
carts operated by successful weekend entrepreneurs are meeting that need and profiting from it. "I started out with a
Nathan's hot dog stand years ago," Mark Sedgley explained,
"and espresso was one of the extras that I served. I began to
notice how popular the espresso was and eventually I decided
to phase out the food! It was a great decision." Mark operates
his espresso cart at three different farmers' markets throughout the week, selling upwards of eight hundred cups on a busy
day—eight hundred cups at $1 apiece!

Two brothers in Oregon are also catering to the national espresso craving with their stand, Dutch Brothers Espresso, in Grants Pass, Oregon. Travis and Dane Boersma were in the dairy business but soon realized that the coffee side of "coffee and cream" was a better bet. Their stand is in the corner of a supermarket parking lot and is popular with weekend shoppers.

Location, Location, Location

Mark stresses the importance of location as an element for success. "Don't sign a lease for a location until you know that it will work. I once had a sidewalk corner spot that had incredibly high traffic flowing by, but nobody ever stopped to buy my espresso!" Parks, beaches, arts and crafts fairs, farmers' markets, movie theaters—there are many places that would be ideal spots for a weekend espresso cart.

Getting Started

Espresso carts are expensive; this is not a business with minimum start-up costs. Fancy espresso carts can cost as much as $20,000. Mark suggests looking for a used cart (but check the water lines first to make sure that it is in good condition) in order to get started, or perhaps buying one in the state of Washington or Oregon. "Carts are much less expensive there, more like $6,000. The wood's cheaper, I guess." A gas-powered cart is the most mobile and would allow you to move around at will. Don't overlook the fact that a permit is required to operate a sidewalk food stand, however, and you should first check with your local authorities about their requirements before you purchase any equipment. What is legal in one county may well be out of code in another, so be very careful.

Educating Yourself

One reason for the growing popularity of espresso stands is that espresso beverages are difficult for consumers to prepare correctly on their own. Like the coffee delivery service detailed in this chapter, operating an espresso cart requires a certain level of expertise in your topic. Develop a taste for the perfect cup. The better your product, the longer the lines standing in front of it at a weekend event! Read books on coffee, talk to experts, and drink, drink, drink, until your espresso palate is developed to the point where you can be certain that your product is of the highest quality.

The Speciality Coffee Association of America (SCAA) forecasts great growth in the coming years for the cart business and estimates the average yearly gross of a full-time cart at $75,000. Ted Lingle, Executive Director of the SCAA, has been quoted as saying that ". . . the cost of a coffee cart, which can be as little as $5,000, is a small percentage of the amount of sales it can generate. [And] coffee carts allow retailers the opportunity to physically move their products outside and into a mall, airport, university, or hospital." The SCAA, in addition to offering material on the coffee business, also has a free 18-page training handout on espresso and cappucino stands.

A Washington-based supplier of espresso carts and related equipment has created a manual to assist entrepreneurs in finding a site for a cart, negotiating a lease, and operating for a successful profit. Contact Burgess Enterprises for more information at (206) 763-0255.

Fresh Juice Bars

Coffee isn't the only thing that Americans are drinking in big gulps; fresh fruit and vegetable juice is another national craze! As a part of the interest in fitness and health, the "juicing" phenomenon has emerged, also due in large part to late-night infomercials featuring the Juiceman. Fresh juice is good for you, and juicing enthusiasts credit juicing with disease prevention and sometimes even cures. But you won't have to make those kinds of claims with your weekend fresh juice stand; just cater to your clients' tastes for delicious fresh juice and squeeze some extra life into your bank account!

Any weekend location that would suit a coffee cart will also suit a fresh juice cart—farmers' markets, country crafts fairs, gardening and home shows, or even a busy street corner are ideal spots for a mobile juice bar. A very successful juice stand at one of the busiest California farmers' markets sells only one kind of juice, delicious homemade lemonade, and the owners have been returning every weekend for years!

Your juice stand should offer at least four varieties of juice, and you will need one juicing machine for each type that you offer (juicers require cleaning between flavors, and this would slow down your production). While the most popular types of juice all feature orange juice as a base, your customers will flip for delicious juice combos.

Tools of the Trade

To run a succeessful weekend juice stand you will need the following:

1. A portable cart that meets health department standards. Before you invest any money in a juice cart, check with your local health department to find out what the standards are for your area. Your cart will need to include a power source to run the juicing machines.

2. Several heavy-duty juicers. There are many brands on the market; make sure that you choose a model that can withstand frequent use.

3. A wholesale source for your fruit. Produce prices sometimes fluctuate according to the weather (which affects a crop's quality and availability) so you will need to be able to adjust your juice prices to reflect this. You would be wise to link up with a source for organic fruit in order to offer your customers organic juice.

4. A terrific location. Choose wisely; your location can mean the difference between astonishing success and expensive failure. Take into account foot traffic, the type of activity in the area, and the typical attendee. The audience for fresh juice is a somewhat upscale one— you will sell more at an organic farmers' market than at a stock car race.

Educating Yourself

To learn more about the health properties of juice and to find recipes for crowd-pleasing juices, this book will be of great help:

> *The Complete Book of Juicing*
> Michael T. Murray, N.D.
> Prima Publishing
> $12.95

"Have Barbecue Will Travel"

California landscape designer Roy Tatman leads a double life—designing gardens for clients during the week, and then custom barbecuing at garden parties on the weekends! "I used to be in the restaurant business," Roy explained, "but when I made a career change I still had all this cooking stuff lying around. So many friends and former customers loved my cooking that I decided to rent out my barbecue skills on the weekends. You don't need a lot of equipment to do this—some tongs and a flipper, maybe a nice red apron. For most parties I use my own two covered kettle barbecues, but if there will be more than 25 guests I spend $30 and rent a big flat grill. My clients are responsible for providing their own tables, chairs, plates, napkins, drinks, and silverware; I just do the food."

Although Roy's business is conducted only on the weekends, there is also a certain amount of advance work that takes place during the week. Picking up groceries and other supplies, prep work on salads and other dishes, and other small errands must be done before the actual event.

Setting Rates

Roy's rates vary according to the menu. "For a basic meal of barbecued steak, beans, and pasta salad I charge $10 per person. It goes up from there, depending on how fancy the host wants to get—appetizers, extra salad offerings, and dessert will bring the price up considerably." Roy advises other barbecue entrepreneurs to watch their profit margin. It is easy to get carried away and end up losing money on the party.

What does it take to start a business like this? Roy recommends it only for folks who already have restaurant and cooking experience and who enjoy working with people. "And don't forget to stand upwind and use a long pair of tongs!" he says.

Specialty Gourmet Products

The fastest-growing section in grocery stores across the country is the specialty gourmet products section, filled with gourmet mustards, dried tomatoes, handmade potato chips, gourmet cookies, and special sauces. One of the attractive features of developing and marketing a specialty gourmet food product is the high price tag attached to it! Customers who shop at gourmet food stores are not looking for bargains, but rather for unique, unusual, and delicious treats that they are quite willing to pay more for. Many of these products are made by hardworking weekend entrepreneurs with a favorite family recipe or creation that they have decided to share with the world.

"My wife's grandfather came over from Cornwall, England, to work in the California gold mines. His mother handed him the family's recipe for shortbread cookies before he left England and told him to fix up a batch whenever he was homesick. The recipe was passed down for generations, and always received rave compliments. Seven months ago, my wife and I decided to test market the cookies to see if they could be sold commercially," Martin Mortenson explained. "And that's how Grandma Pearlie's Shortbread was born."

Working with their teenage daughter Shannon, Martin and his wife, Gail, found a local baker who was willing to rent them the bakery ovens during off hours. "Without her help we never would have done it. The investment in space and professional equipment would have been too high." Baking Wednesday evenings and Sunday afternoons, the Mortensons produce their shortbread cookies in large batches to satisfy the ever-growing demand on the retail level.

The Real Costs of Business

Every month their business has grown in size, but Martin, a full-time computer salesman, doubts that they will grow Grandma Pearlie's Shortbread into a full-time business. "It is a very labor-intensive business; but since it's the family doing it, we save on labor costs. If we had to go out and hire other people to help, it would be a different game entirely." Paying employee Social Security taxes, disability insurance, and other time-intensive administrative matters that arise when employing others take both time and money away from a small business like this, quickly eating into the profit. The biggest expense for the Mortensons so far has been a $1 million liability insurance policy that they took out before they brought their product onto the market. Other large costs include state licensing fees and local business fees. "But we're having fun," Martin adds. "That's the key thing."

Success Factors

The main factors for success in the specialty foods market are the uniqueness and the quality of your product. Once you find a niche to fill you must then test market it to evaluate the product before you sink large sums of money into it. The Mortensons sent samples to a wide circle of friends and included evaluation postcards to be filled out and returned with honest opinions. Gail Mortenson also gave away samples of the shortbread at a specialty store to test the opinions of total strangers. Attractive and professional-looking packaging for your product is also an important element. A homey touch is sometimes nice, but customers in gourmet shops are looking for a certain amount of sophistication in their food.

Handling Distribution

While it is possible for part-time specialty food product entrepreneurs to handle local distribution of their product on their
own, to expand statewide or nationwide, professional distribu-
tors must be found. Ask the merchandise buyers at local
gourmet food stores for the names of specialty product distrib-
utors. A distributor will charge a percentage of your sales, but
the increased business should make it worthwhile.

Karen Jackson of Karen's Mustard suggests, "Another
way to handle distribution is to go to the food shows and find
other small businesses with gourmet products who might form
a distribution network with you. They could sell your product
with their own in their area, while you distribute their product
along with yours in your area. It is a good way to increase your
effectiveness."

Karen went into business selling mustard made from a
recipe that her dad, Herb Jackson, created. She warns that anyone going into this type of business will need to have some free
time available during the week to make sales calls with merchandise buyers, who simply aren't available on the weekends. A gourmet food producer's weekends are spent either
demonstrating their product in stores that carry it (giving away
samples to customers) or selling their product direct to the public at crafts fairs or farmers' markets.

On a Smaller Scale

There are several levels of seriousness in the specialty food
market. On a smaller scale than either Grandma Pearlie's Shortbread or Karen's Mustard, Pat, a school secretary, makes and
sells her own specially created champagne jelly at Christmas
bazaars and to her colleagues at school during the holiday season. "I noticed that lots of people bring things to school to sell,
so I decided that I would too. For years I'd been making a
recipe for champagne jelly that I had created by combining two
other recipes. Everyone seemed to like it, so I realized that I
already had a popular product on my hands. Every December

I take special orders and also make up enough to sell at two or three crafts boutiques. Over the course of the season I make enough money to buy all of my Christmas gifts! It's been a big help to my budget."

Educating Yourself

To learn more about what types of products are already on the market and what seems to be missing, the industry magazine *Fancy Food* is a good source of information. Call Talcott Publishing at (312) 664-4040 for subscription information. Once you decide to learn more, you should attend one of the gourmet products industry shows that are held several times a year around the country. For more information call the shows' producers, the National Association for the Specialty Food Trade (NASFT), at (212) 921-1690.

According to the NASFT, the specialty food industry is growing and thriving. A recent survey revealed that consumers short on large sums of disposable income are ". . . finding more gratification in pasta than Porsches." So now is definitely the time to get revved up and start your own specialty product. Start rummaging through old family recipe card files—perhaps there is a secret recipe that can cook up a profit for you!

Thinking It Through

Food preparation is a tricky field, and a much-regulated one. Whenever food is involved that will be consumed by the public, each individual city, county, and state gets in on the act. You must investigate the regulations in your area before starting any food-related venture. In addition to health regulations you will have to take into consideration the following:

1. **Licenses.** You must meet the regulations and standards in your area. Needless to say, there are fees involved.

2. **Product liability.** "Why take chances?" advises Martin Mortenson of Grandma Pearlie's Shortbread. In this litigious society it is

wise to be protected against the possibility of a lawsuit. Speak to your insurance broker about liability insurance.

3. **Custom kitchens.** Building a kitchen that meets the health standards is not an inexpensive undertaking. It is possible to rent space in a custom kitchen to get started. Check for ads in local newspapers and magazines that cater to "foodies." In the San Francisco Bay Area, for example, *BAYFOOD* magazine occasionally carries ads from commercial kitchens with space available on an hourly basis. Many churches have professional kitchens. You might start on a small scale by checking to see if you can rent time in a church kitchen.

4. **Taste and quality.** These are two factors that you must not skimp on if you plan to become a success in the food business. Invest a great deal of time and patience in developing your product so that what you bring to market is of the highest quality and the best possible taste. Fancy packaging may sell your product once, but taste and quality will keep your customers coming back again and again.

5. **Expenses and start-up costs.** Starting a specialty food business from scratch is not cheap; neither is buying an espresso cart or other weekend food stand. Before you launch yourself into the wonderful world of food, please consider how much it will cost to get started, and how long it will take before you can realistically expect to see a return on your investment. If you need a fast-money SAM, the food business is not for you.

In lieu of a fancy (and expensive) professional kitchen, you can also hire a "co-producer" to produce your product for you. These are food development and production companies who can produce your mustard, honey spread, marmalade, or other specialty product in large quantities at wholesale prices. The minimum run is generally 250 cases of product. To find a co-producer in your area, you can ask other small-time specialty food entrepreneurs or look for advertisements in professional food magazines.

Brainstorm on Trends

In the gourmet food business, as in other types of businesses, it is important to keep an eye on trends. If you don't already have an idea for a gourmet food product, why don't you brainstorm on some of these current trends:

- **Meatless eating.** Everyone is eating less red meat nowadays. Why not develop a weekend food stand that caters to this desire?

- **Low-fat foods.** Along with less red meat, we are also working hard to lower our fat intake. Many favorite foods like muffins are now showing up in fat-reduced or fat-free versions. What can you develop in a fat-free way?

- **Gourmet teas.** Coffee is already hot, but gourmet tea is not far behind! Check out the new teas from Republic of Tea (the new brainchild of the folks who developed Banana Republic) and Royal Tea. These entrepreneurs are at the forefront of a growing interest in very expensive upscale imported teas. There is a way for weekend entrepreneurs to cash in. Perhaps a tea stand or a tea-tasting club? Think about it.

- **International food.** Thai, Indian, Caribbean—our taste buds are going international and there is still plenty of room for entrepreneurs to develop international food stands, spice and flavoring packages, sauces, and specialty cookbooks.

Gourmet foods and food-related products can be a terrifically profitable and fun business. So roll up your sleeves, go into your kitchen, and get creative! Who knows where you can go!

Chapter Nine

Long Shots— Great Ideas for Special People

Here are ideas that are terrific, but won't work for just anyone, anywhere. These SAMs require special talents (like writing and publishing), special locations (gold mining country or tourist areas), or special knowledge (books and literature). Each of these business ideas is a real cash bonanza if you have all of the special ingredients to make it work!

Big-Time Profits from Small-Time Publishing

I have been working in the world of books for some ten years now, and I have had the chance to observe many different styles and types of publishing. As I mentioned in the beginning pages of this book, since 1989 I have been self-publishing a small booklet that I wrote about an inexpensive way to travel. Over the years I have sold several thousand copies of my book, *The Air Courier's Handbook*. At 44 pages, the book is far too small to be carried in bookstores and my only sales outlet has been mail order. Glamorous as the prospect of being published by a big publishing house may seem to an author, I must say that my "small-time" publishing project is far more personally profitable than most standard publishing arrangements. Not only is it unusually profitable, it was not at all hard to do! Read on, and I will show you how anyone with writing skills can find a successful topic, publish a booklet, and market it for an impressive SAM.

A Cheaper Way to Fly

Several years ago my friend Sherry Miller moved to Indonesia, a very expensive plane ride away from my home base of northern California. Remembering that in college I had heard that traveling as an air courier was a cheap way to fly, I set about to investigate. My big break came the night I overheard a conversation in a restaurant about air courier travel and boldly interrupted to learn more. And what I learned was valuable indeed, so valuable that I took all of my new information and set about to research and write a book about air courier travel to fill a gaping information hole for budget-minded travelers.

Just the Facts, Ma'am

My original plan was to write a book of 75 to 80 pages, hire a designer to achieve the right "look," and send it off to a short-run printer for a run of two or three thousand perfect-bound books. After all, I was a book publishing professional and had my reputation to think of! During the time that I was working on my manuscript, I attended a writer's conference in the seaside town of Carmel. I spent the lunch hour sitting across from a woman who had written a booklet about hydroponic farming that she was successfully marketing through small ads in the back of magazines like *Mother Jones* and *Whole Earth*. Her booklet was a pretty basic 12-page, photocopied and stapled piece of work, and she was most anxious for my professional editorial opinion. I held her booklet in my hands, opened my mouth to speak, and promptly shut it. In seconds I had been struck by an incredible revelation.

I had been on the verge of suggesting that she upgrade the appearance of her work, spend a bit more money on design and production to achieve a more professional look. And the thunderbolt idea that struck me mute was this—excessive money spent on design and production for a mail-order book is a waste of money. Readers of her ad in *Mother Jones* were strictly interested in her INFORMATION; that was the only thing that they were seeking. Information, pure and simple, instead of a fancy book to put on a shelf. Books that are produced for the mail-order market need to be heavy on information but do not necessarily need to be professionally produced. Your customer will be very happy with the information, and you will be very happy with the improved profits!

The Air Courier's Handbook

Using this newly discovered information, I set about rethinking my air courier book. I scaled down my original idea of the length, dropped all plans for hiring a designer, and tossed the short-run printers' brochures in the trash. After several weeks of work, this is what I produced: *The Air Courier's Handbook: Travel the World on a Shoestring,* by Jennifer Basye—a 44-page stapled booklet filled with all the knowledge you need to travel as an air courier, as well as phone numbers of air courier companies and their flight destinations. It is decorated with cartoons and illustrations by my brother, Paul Basye; the cover is designed with noncopyrighted clip-art. This booklet cost a little over $1 each to produce; I sell it through the mail for $10. Instead of printing up 2,000 copies all at once, I just go to the local copy shop and have the book made up in batches of 250 at a time, greatly reducing the money I have tied up in inventory. After also subtracting for the cost of an envelope and postage, I make somewhere in the neighborhood of $8 profit for every book sold. With the extra money that I have made from this book I have taken two trips to Asia in the past two years, trips that I could not otherwise have afforded. Naturally, I flew as an air courier!

Getting Started

How can you do this, too? I think that with careful planning it is possible for anyone with average writing skills to create a booklet that will sell well through mail order.

Finding a valuable topic that will produce sales is the first step. *Saving money* and *making money* are far and away the two best topics for a mail-order booklet that works; food and recipes are also popular. Every day you come across small pieces of information that, properly packaged, could form the basis for a good booklet. Look carefully around your life— what (or whom) do you know? Do you have a time- or money-saving trick that would save hours each week? Millions of people buy books on housecleaning tips; just ask author Don Aslett. Have you developed endless ways to keep small children occupied and quiet hour after hour? Just think how many harried mothers would love to know your secret. Has your recipe for caramel fudge been sought after by friends and relatives? Page after page of small classified ads for recipes appear each week in the *National Enquirer,* so someone must be buying them!

Good ideas are all around you and could pop into your mind at any time. While working on the "foraging" section of this book, I came to realize that there is an opportunity for a booklet, "Secrets of a Successful Forager" or "Money on the Forest Floor," something along those lines. Keep your eyes and your ears open at all times for ideas. If you know how to research a topic you can write about anything. What about a small travel booklet that lists hotels in Europe that offer discounts for senior citizens? Think of the size of the potential market for that one!

Brainstorming Ideas

To get your creative juices flowing and help you discover an idea that will work for you, sit down with a blank piece of paper and begin to brainstorm with these terms:

101 Ways to . . .

An Artist's Guide to . . .

Time-Saving Tips on . . .

Never Spend Money Again on . . .

The Beach Lover's Guide to . . .

A Woman's Guide to . . .

Love Secrets of . . .

A Parent's Guide to . . .

A Hiker's Guide to . . .

The Money-Saving Guide to . . .

The Complete Traveler's Guide to . . .

The Insider's Guide to . . .

The Retiree's Handy Guide to . . .

The Romantic's Guide to . . .

Well, you get the idea; the possibilities are endless.

Checklist for Success

Once you arrive at an idea, make sure that the topic you choose meets these criteria:

1. **Large potential audience.**   How many people would be interested in this booklet? Can my target group (parents, nurses, pilots, and so on) afford to buy this booklet?

2. **Compelling topic.**   What is it about this booklet that would inspire my target audience to buy it? Will they save money, time, or really learn something that can improve their lives?

3. **Researchable topic.**   Do I know enough already, or can I research this topic thoroughly and really deliver what I promise in the title?

4. **Targeted media.**   Is there a good way to reach my target audience? What newspapers and magazines might they read? Will these papers review or write about my booklet?

If you can answer "yes" to all of these questions, then the topic you have chosen has a very good chance of succeeding as a mail-order book or booklet. The next step, of course, is to research and write the book! Don't make it longer than it has to be (you will waste money), but don't cheat your readers. Deliver what you promise and more.

Producing Your Book

In years past, the cost of producing a professional-looking book or booklet was prohibitive, but with the ever-increasing availability of desktop publishing it is now possible for you to create a quality product on your own. Many copy shops and desktop publishing establishments allow you to rent their equipment on an hourly basis and work on your project at their own facility. The store employees can help you learn your way around a desktop publishing program, and there are also several good books on the market that will teach you the skills you need. In a matter of hours you can produce a great-looking book that will present your information in a clear, readable, and easily accessible style. Don't get too carried away on the design. When it comes time to print copies of your book, you should start off by ordering only small quantities. Now, on to the next step—selling that book!

Selling Your Book

If you have chosen your topic wisely by concentrating on a compelling topic that has a large and affluent potential audience who read newspapers and magazines, then marketing and selling your book should be easy. Let's study the example of *The Air Courier's Handbook.*

Targeted to adventurous world travelers looking for an inexpensive way to travel, my first sales method was to place ads in small off-beat travel magazines like *Great Expeditions* or *International Travel News.* The cost of advertising was inexpensive and I was assured that I was sending my message out to the right group of potential customers. Each one of these ads was a modest success; in each instance I made twice as much money in book sales as I'd spent on the cost of the ad. I did this for the first year and sold several hundred copies.

In my second year of business, I had grown more comfortable with my product (I kept expecting people to complain about the size; instead, I got fan mail on what a great source of hard-to-find info it was!) and more confident about my knowledge of the topic. I wrote a press release about *The Air Courier's Handbook* and sent several dozen copies and sample books off to travel editors at newspapers and magazines around the country. The reaction was incredible! Over the course of a year, I received several big write-ups in the travel sections of major newspapers like the *Boston Globe* and the *San Francisco Chronicle* and the orders just poured in.

There was one heady period of time when I would find 30 or more book orders per day in my post office box—$300 per day in extra income. Unfortunately that only lasted for a few weeks; but since then stories have appeared regularly about my little book (I update the book every year and send press releases and sample books out every time), and I average between 10 and 15 orders a week.

My costs for this publicity campaign are limited to postage and the hard costs of the book (around $1 each) and the rewards have been extraordinary. Free publicity is much, much more effective than paid advertising. At every step, as you produce your booklet, you should be considering not only the needs and expectations of your customers but how the media will view your book. If you send out a professional product that is newsworthy, you can get publicity. If you send out a shoddy little book on a topic of no interest, then an editor will pitch it in the trash.

Educating Yourself

Self-publishing is a very rewarding experience, both emotionally and financially. Choose your topic wisely, produce a good product, and enjoy the fruits of your labor. My business address is listed here, and I would be happy to give you my opinion on your booklet idea. Send me a letter about your project and I will respond with my honest reaction about the potential success. And if you would like to see an example of "small-time publishing," just send me $10 and I will send you a copy of *The Air Courier's Handbook* at cost. You can reach me by writing to to me care of Prima Publishing, P.O. Box 1260, Rocklin, CA 95677. Happy publishing!

To learn more about how to put together a book like this, I recommend:

> *Publishing Short-Run Books: How to Paste Up and Re-produce Books Instantly Using Your Quick Print Shop*
> Dan Poynter
> Para Publications
> $5.95

Bike Rentals

What better way for tourists to spend a beautiful day on the coast than biking slowly along a scenic road until the sun sets, stopping whenever they like to take in the view and have an impromptu picnic . . . but unless they packed their bikes in with their luggage it's only a dream. Only a dream until you open up a weekend bike rental business, that is!

Domestic tourism is up in all areas of the country, and many new tourist destinations are emerging. If you were far-sighted enough to settle in one of these places, or if there is not already a bike rental business in your tourist town, get busy and start one. Every weekend you could be making money while happy tourists pedal around on your bikes taking in the sights.

Getting Started

It is not necessary to have very expensive equipment or a fancy location to start this business. Unless the terrain of your town requires mountain bikes, you are better off buying old balloon-tire route bikes, basic one- or two-speed models from the 60s, and simple children's bikes to use as rentals. Paint them all a highly identifiable color; make sure that the tires and the brakes are in good condition; buy simple bicycle locks for the customers to use for the afternoon; and you are all set.

You will not be needing a fancy storefront for your business; the side parking lot of another business will do just fine.

Make sure that you are located on the most popular street in the town, preferably one with high foot-traffic. Approach the owner of a shop that you think is well-situated and ask if you can rent a corner of the shop's parking lot on the weekends. You will need only enough space to set up a few bike stands and a sandwich board or sign to advertise your rental service. What could be simpler?

Finding Customers

In addition to attracting rental customers from the foot traffic passing by on the street, you should approach local hotels and bed & breakfasts to let them know bike rentals are available. They could steer customers your way and might be interested enough to rent a few bikes themselves from you on the weekends for their guests to use. Printing up a supply of simple brochures or flyers to leave in the lobbies would be a wise move, as would alerting the local tourist board to your new business.

Tie-in Services

If you care to take this one step further, you could also develop bicycle tours of your area. Read "Odds and Ends," Chapter 7, for information about designing and leading custom tours. Another related (although more complicated) idea is to develop a bicycle pedicab service in your tourist town. Not recommended for hilly areas, this is a popular service in the southern California town of Westwood and in several other tourist towns.

Book Scout

"There are some book scouts who stop by every two weeks with eight big boxes of books and leave with around $500," used bookstore employee Gina Lewis told me. "Once I developed an understanding of the business, I started to do it too. Walking home from a friend's house one day, I stopped by a garage sale, spent $8.50, and later that afternoon made $37 by selling those same books at a used bookstore." Not bad for an afternoon stroll, and a fine way for book lovers to make a little extra money on the weekends.

Not every book can be resold for profit to a used bookstore. Before you rush out to hit every garage and yard sale you can find, you should first familiarize yourself with what types of books your local used bookstores are interested in. Some used bookstores specialize in metaphysical books, collectible cookbooks, or travel literature, and others stock general interest titles. Chances are that there are several used bookstores in your area, each with its own personality and specialized need. "The best way to learn is just by doing it," Gina advises. "And you will learn a lot from the buyer in the bookstore. As they go through the books you have brought in they will probably explain why they won't take this book or that book, because this one is too old, and they already have several copies of that one."

What to Look For

To give you a basic understanding of the kinds of books that you should keep an eye out for at flea markets or garage and yard sales, here is a brief list of valuable categories of books:

- **Hardcover cookbooks.** The newer the better, but there is a market for older titles as well.

- **Classic children's books.** Hardcover, illustrated books are the most valuable for collectors but are also the most difficult to find on a garage sale table.

- **Current hardcover fiction.** The newest Danielle Steel? Sure, pay 25¢ for it and you will be able to sell it to a used bookstore for up to 30% of the list price.

- **Hardcover horror and fantasy fiction.** There are book scouts out there who can now send their children to college on the money they have made from early first edition Stephen King novels. I know a policeman who supplements his income with collectible horror books; he suggests also watching for books by Clive Barker and Dean Koontz.

- **Antique and collectible historical books.** There is a steady market for early California books and for old books about most states and regions. In California the most collectible books are those on the "Zamarano Eighty;" uncovering one at an estate sale will reap large rewards.

- **Early metaphysical and occult works.** Books by Edgar Cayce or Aleister Crowley, books on astrology or the Tao, and any other type of metaphysical book are very collectible.

- **Trade paperback literature.** Trade paperbacks are paperback books that are somewhat larger than the mass-market pocket paperbacks. Works of fiction in this size can easily be resold to used bookstores. Don't pay more than 25¢ each at the garage sale, and you should be able to at least triple your money at the used bookstore.

- **First edition fiction.** Older works by Fitzgerald, Faulkner, and Hemingway are very valuable, but so are newer works of fiction. In Chicago, for instance, first editions of mystery writer Sara Paretsky fetch very high prices. Keep your eyes open and you will discover amazing prizes! I once bought a first edition Hemingway in very fine condition for $75.

Once you get in the habit of scouting for collectible books, you will be hooked. As a confirmed book lover, I search constantly for books both to keep (I kept the Hemingway) and to sell. A related way to make extra money with used books is to buy leather-bound books to resell to interior decorators. Believe it or not, there are shallow folks out there who just want a shelf full of impressive leather-bound books that are meant to be a part of the decorating scheme! Talk to interior decorators to see if there is a market for "books-by-the-yard" in your area before you get started.

Niche Newsletters

Another potential publishing profit-maker is found in the burgeoning field of niche newsletters. Once seldom seen, newsletters are cropping up all over to address all types of topics. If you read the section on herb farming in Chapter 3, you know that there is a newsletter that goes to folks who grow herbs for profit. There are also newsletters for diverse groups like emergency room nurses, retired firefighters, and snowboarders.

Book Bound

James Meek and Debra Lilly started their monthly newsletter, *Book Bound,* to fill an information hole that they had identified. "Here in northern California we discovered that a lot of the timely information about authors appearing in bookstores or at readings was simply slipping through the cracks. We are both avid readers and followers of the literary scene; so we figured that if we were missing the information, then there must be a pretty big group out there that was also missing it." And so *Book Bound,* "A Newsletter for Readers," was born in an effort to inform the literary communities in Sacramento, Stockton, Davis, Folsom, and Elk Grove of scheduled events.

Book Bound is distributed free to the reading public in bookstores and libraries. James and Debra sell advertising to defray the cost of publishing and sell the newsletters themselves to bookstores for 10¢ per copy (libraries receive it free). "Bookstores can buy 500 copies of *Book Bound* for $50 and give them away as a goodwill gesture to their customers. It is a very low-cost way for them to add an extra service to their business."

Getting Started

Before launching *Book Bound,* James and Debra went on a fact-finding mission that serves as a good example of the process you should undergo before deciding that newsletter publishing is right for you. "First we sent questionnaires to bookstores outlining the idea for *Book Bound* and asking for early suggestions and feedback. Of the questionnaires we sent out we probably got about half back, so that gave us a good basic understanding of how it might be received in the marketplace. We put together a simple sample issue, complete with dummy ads, and then actually went into the bookstores to start talking to them about both advertising and distribution. That produced real results, and now after just seven months we are up to a circulation of 1,000 copies available through 40 locations."

Newsletters targeted to small audience niches should be well designed and readable, but needn't be extravagantly designed or overly colorful. Many beginning publishers get sidetracked into trying to produce a fancy newsletter when a modest one will do. *Book Bound* is eight pages long, two legal-sized pieces of recycled paper folded in half. "We tried to give it a literary look," James says of their design. "We didn't start with much money, and we tried hard to keep our costs low by making an attractive but simple newsletter." And they succeeded. If you would like to take a look at *Book Bound* to get an idea of how they did it, feel free to write for a free sample copy:

Book Bound
c/o River City Word Shop
P.O. Box 160963
Sacramento, California 95816-0963

Travel Unlimited

A different type of newsletter is produced in Allston, Massachusetts, by Steve Lantos. His monthly newsletter, *Travel Unlimited,* serves to keep air couriers informed with up-to-the-minute intelligence on prices of courier flights and other cheap air travel around the world. Because I update my book *The Air Courier's Handbook* (see previous section, *Big-Time Profits from Small-Time Publishing*) only once a year, I subscribe to Steve's newsletter to keep abreast of courier trends.

At $25 per year for a subscription, the newsletter has subscribers scattered around the world. Unlike the typeset and designed giveaway newsletter *Book Bound, Travel Unlimited* is produced by Steve on a typewriter. Each issue consists of two pages of typed information copied and stapled. No advertising is included, just good solid information. Not the most elegant newsletter, but the information is so valuable to his readers that no one has ever complained!

The Tightwad Gazette

Sometimes a small newsletter will hit it big. That's what happened to Amy Dacyczyn and her newsletter *The Tightwad Gazette*. Amy started her newsletter as a way to spread the word about living a frugal life (reusing vacuum cleaner bags, making soap last longer, and buying oats for baking from animal feed stores!). The media picked up on it, and she has now hit it big with both her newsletter and a bestselling book based on her ideas. So you never know where your small newsletter might lead you!

A Niche Is Born

What kind of newsletter does the world need? Flip back to the section on *Big-Time Profits from Small-Time Publishing;* many of the same standards and criteria that a booklet needs to meet also apply to a niche newsletter. How large is the potential audience? Are they already served by a newsletter or magazine? Can you do a better job? Become a keen observer of the world and its trends and you will soon develop a knack for spotting a potential audience. Some hardworking entrepreneurs in Oakland have started a newsletter for karaoke lovers! In Chapter 8, "Cooking Up Dollars," I describe the tremendous interest in gourmet coffees and the growing interest in gourmet teas. There is a hole in the market for newsletters that cater to coffee and tea lovers. Travel articles about coffee plantations in exotic places, tasting comparisons, recommendations, recipes, and more could be covered in such a newsletter. Get started now and be sure to send me a copy when you are finished!

Educating Yourself

Three resource books that will help you get started are:

> *Newsletter Sourcebook*
> Mark Beach
> North Light Books
> $26.95
>
> *Publishing Newsletters*
> Howard Penn Hudson
> Macmillan
> $13.95
>
> *Publish Magazines and Newspapers with a Macintosh Computer*
> Harris Smith
> Upper River
> $16.95

Used Jeans, Vintage and Collectible Clothing

"It's a fashion thing," says Jim Goodykoontz, when I asked him to explain the craze for used jeans and collectible clothing. "In Japan and Europe and other places they know more about Levi-Strauss than most Americans do. Purely American stuff, they just go crazy for it." Jim started to develop an interest in vintage clothing while working as a park ranger in California. "I got transferred to the Governor's Mansion museum in Sacramento, and I found out that if I dressed in vintage clothing I could get out of wearing the standard-issue ranger's uniform. So I started to look around at what was available." He started out looking for turn-of-the-century men's clothing, and slowly his collection grew to include all manner of vintage clothing.

Jim also began to notice how much vintage clothing dealers would pay for the things he found, and a SAM was quickly developed!

The big craze nowadays is for used jeans. The jeans are sent overseas to be sold for much higher prices than they fetch here in America. Not just used Levi's but old Lee and Wrangler jeans are worth money to a used jeans dealer. "There is a ready market for used 501s. They sell for anywhere from $35 to $60 out of the country, and there are dealers all over who are combing the countryside looking for jeans to buy. Most big cities are pretty much glutted with dealers, but small towns and out-of-the-way spots should be a great place to go looking," Jim suggests. "By getting up early to hit the garage sales, it is still possible for an energetic person to make anywhere from $300 to $800 a month with used jeans."

What to Look For

The overseas market is crazy for other vintage-Americana clothing besides old jeans. Keep your eyes peeled for any of the following items:

- old leather motorcycle jackets
- WWII leather bomber jackets
- Air Force or Army nylon bomber jackets
- old Hawaiian shirts (40s and 50s)
- vintage bowling shirts
- old fancy western clothing
- vintage men's formal wear
- any fancy men's stuff from the 50s (Jim described it as "the kind of stuff Ricky Ricardo would wear")

Jim predicts that the next big thing will be clothing from the 70s, so you might also start keeping an eye out for platform shoes and bell-bottoms. And if you are successful in finding any of the listed items, then what do you do? Why, you can call Jim Goodykoontz, of course. "I'd love to buy stuff from people all across the country. California is getting pretty tapped out, but I know that there are closets all across America that contain valuable things." Call Jim at (916) 442-5342 and tell him what you've found. But remember, you've got to get up pretty early to hit those garage sales before your competitors do!

Weekend Gold Prospector

The United States is the fourth-largest gold producer in the world, ranked just behind South Africa, the former Soviet Union, and Canada. Although there have been several gold booms around the country throughout its history, scientific satellite photo-imaging technology reveals that previous mining has only scratched the surface of America's gold and that 75% to 85% of the wealth has yet to be discovered! What better way to participate in a fascinating old pastime while at the same time making extra money. In many parts of the country there really is "gold in them thar' hills!" And at a current price of $388.00 an ounce, it is well worth your time to go look for it!

Where to Look

Where is the gold? A simple question with a multitude of answers. The major gold-prospecting states are as follows: California, Colorado, South Dakota, Alaska, Nevada, Utah, Montana, Idaho, Washington, Arkansas, New Mexico, Wyoming, North and South Carolina, Georgia, Virginia, Alabama, and Oregon. Each of these states has the proper geological composition for gold and has undergone a gold boom at sometime in its history. Even states that have been heavily mined, as California was during the 49er period, are continuing to produce large gold discoveries for commercial mines and weekend prospectors. During the winter of 1993, a commercial gold mine in the town of Jamestown uncovered a nugget of gold weighing some 60 pounds! Workers weren't quite sure what it was when they saw it coming down the conveyor belt.

Getting Started

If you live in a state that does have gold, how then do you find it? Most towns near gold fields have mining equipment and supply stores that are staffed with helpful fellow prospectors who are happy to chew the fat about new and hot areas for gold prospecting. They can sell you the simple supplies you need to get started (an inexpensive gold pan, a shovel, a hand-pick, crevice tools, a bucket, coffee cans, a garden trowel, small glass vials to store the gold flakes, tweezers, a magnifying glass, and a magnet) as well as topographical maps and locally published books on the best areas to prospect. The local Bureau of Land Management can also help provide maps as well as advice and information on staking mining claims.

Most weekend gold prospectors start out simply, using the gold-panning method. This is the least expensive and least equipment-intensive method and is generally done at the stream bank in an area where gold is likely to have collected. More complicated prospecting techniques that you might graduate to include using a sluice or rocker box, operating a hydraulic concentrator, or running a small dredge.

A Family SAM

Weekend gold prospecting is a terrific and fun SAM for the whole family to work on. What better way for your children to learn about your state's early history than to bend over and pan the same stream that old-time miners worked 100 years ago? And what better way for a married couple to work together than to stand waist-deep in a cold stream operating a dredge? Of course, you may fight over just how you will be using the first few nuggets that you find—perhaps mounted as a necklace for the wife or a heavy handsome ring for the husband? I'll leave that decision up to you! Once you have enough gold to sell, look in the Yellow Pages for a refiner of precious metals. The staff at the mining shop will also be able to steer you toward outlets who will buy your gold.

Educating Yourself

The best book on the topic is an incredibly well-written and easy-to-understand book (how do you think I got started?) called:

> *Gold! Gold! A Beginner's Handbook and Recreational Guide: How and Where to Prospect for Gold!*
> Joseph F. Petralia
> Sierra Outdoor Products
> P.O. Box 2497
> San Francisco, California 94126
> $9.95

This same company also sells mining supplies by mail order, if you are not able to find an equipment store in your area. For more information you can also contact the Gold Prospectors Association of America at P.O. Box 507, Bonsall, California 92003.

Worm Farming

Throughout history, wonderful things have been said about the lowly worm. Cleopatra called the worm "a sacred animal"; Aristotle said that worms were the "guts of the soil"; and Darwin said that they were "more powerful than the African elephant and more important to the economy than the cow"! And as it turns out, worms are also a way to earn a darn good living!

City Worms and Compost

Cindy Nelson is the owner of City Worms & Compost in San Francisco. She does a brisk business selling wooden worm boxes for composting food waste to home recyclers. "Well, I make and sell worm boxes large enough to handle the garbage of one person, two people, or four people. You feed them your food waste, you see, and they eat it and in turn make a wonderfully fine soil that you can use in your garden." Cindy's wooden worm boxes are not cheap; she builds them out of exterior-grade plywood and her customers pay from $45 for the one-person box to $110 for the four-person box. And that does not include the worms!

Red worms are the key element. Red worms are voracious eaters of waste; one pound of worms will eat one-half pound of food waste per day. With the spotlight on landfill and garbage nowadays, many cities across the country are mandating that waste be reduced, and worms are a trendy way to do this. "This is definitely a growth area for entrepreneurs," Cindy advises, "and building and selling worm boxes is ideal for part-time income." Cindy alerted many environmental, composting, and recycling groups to her worm boxes and these groups do much of her publicity for her—passing out her brochures, recommending her service, and steering customers her way.

Although she originally planned to only build boxes, the red worms have been in such demand that Cindy has also started a small worm farm in her backyard. "I have two raised beds of 10" rows, and I feed the worms manure. I sell worms for $12 per pound (subtracting the weight of the earth!), and then if my customer wants me to set up the worm box, I will do it for a $15 set-up fee. I coat the inside of the worm box with vegetable oil and add a layer of shredded newspaper and just a handful of soil. Once the worms start eating garbage they produce "castings," very enriched soil. Lots of my customers put the worm box under the sink and feed the worms there, but others put it out in the yard. The boxes have hinged lids and are pretty sturdy; you could use it for a bench if you wanted to."

Educating Yourself

Cindy learned about worms and worm boxes by attending a "master composter training program" offered in her area. She suggests contacting the local office in your area that deals with recycling, garbage, or waste removal, and inquiring about composting classes. Gardening groups as well might teach worm composting. She also recommends two books to help beginners understand more about worms and learn to build the boxes:

Worms Eat My Garbage
Mary Appelhoff
Flower Press
10332 Shaver Road
Kalamazoo, Michigan 49002
$8.95

What Every Gardener Should Know About Earthworms
Dr. Henry Hopp
Storey/Garden Way Publishing
$2.95

Thinking It Through

What's to think through? You pretty much have to wing it on these ideas, much the same way as with the "Odds and Ends" opportunities discussed in Chapter 6. These ideas all require very special components—talent, creativity, imagination, guts, knowledge, craziness, location, and stick-to-itiveness. Chances are that if you are missing just one of these ingredients, then the idea will not work. Please be very clear-eyed in your self-assessment before you launch yourself into one of these long shots. The payoffs are terrific, but failure is no fun for anyone.

This is, needless to say, my own favorite chapter. I believe our country was built by people willing to take a long shot on a crazy idea—an idea about harnessing electricity, about developing a telephone, about building a personal computer. I certainly don't count myself among these lofty inventors, but I do believe that anyone who tries out an unusual idea and tries to make it work has a right to be proud. Don't let your friends, your family, or your spouse try to make you feel silly when you turn on your computer to compose your first issue of your niche newsletter. Ignore your family's snickers as you wake up early every Saturday morning to go off to neighborhood yard sales in search of used blue jeans and collectible books. Hold your head high, and be proud that you are taking a chance in life instead of sitting around complaining about how much better things should be!

Chapter Ten

Moms at Home— Extra Money for Entrepreneurial Mothers

We all know just how much work stay-at-home moms do day in and day out, but the darned shame of it is that no one pays us! But for those many moms who would like to build up an extra nest egg or contribute to the household income, there are countless ways to stay at home with the kids and make money while you are there! Many of the women that I have interviewed throughout this book are full-time moms who have discovered truly inventive ways to make extra cash. I made it a point to ask each of them which of the business ideas in this book were the best suited to moms at home, and this chapter lists the top suggestions from these entrepreneurial experts! The ideas presented here are in capsule form; for the full description of each business and how to succeed in it, please turn to the complete listing.

Top Ten Weekend Businesses for Moms

1. Herb farming.   Herbs are big business and getting bigger all the time. Tending an herb-farming business in your backyard is an ideal pursuit for a full-time mom. The garden and its plants can be cared for throughout the week as a part of your regular at-home routine. Deliveries to accounts can be managed while the kids are in school, or the kids can even go with you and learn about business at your side! If you run a stand at a farmers' market on the weekends, they can easily come along for the morning (the markets seldom last all day) or spend a day hanging out with Dad. You can find a more complete description and sources of information on herb farming in Chapter 3, "Old-Fashioned Money."

2. Cut flower business.   Much like herb farming, growing cut flowers is perfect for moms. Perhaps you should even combine the two pursuits so that you can sell upscale bouquets that mix herbs and flowers. What a wonderfully rewarding way to spend time at home—taking care of your children and your beautiful flower garden at the same time, knowing that both children and flowers will reward you hundreds of times over. The fresh flower business is fully detailed in Chapter 3, "Old-Fashioned Money."

3. Hand-rolled beeswax candles.   This is my favorite money-making craft, and I do it to great success on the weekends. You can roll candles late into the night when your children are sleeping. Each candle takes only seconds to make and sells for a terrific profit. And you get the added bonus of a pleasant beeswax smell pervading the room while you work. A steady source of crafts fairs is schools and day-care centers, so you may find that it is not hard at all to find opportunities to sell your wares to your friends and fellow moms. You also get to decorate your own home inexpensively with very posh-looking beeswax candles. Look in Chapter 5, "Crafty Business," for the rundown on this business idea.

4. Antiques and collectibles dealer.   Most antique galleries require very little in the way of actual work hours; maintaining a small space in a cooperative gallery might require you to be there as few as four hours per month. The rest of the time you can scout out estate sales, flea markets, and yard sales looking for bargain wares to resell in your space. Find out more about this rewarding business idea in Chapter 3, "Old-Fashioned Money."

5. Christmas bazaars and open house crafts boutiques. A terrific way to earn extra money around the holidays, organizing Christmas bazaars and crafts boutiques is also an awful lot of fun. Much of your organizing can be done while the children are at school or asleep, so full-time moms do find that this works well with their other commitments. Once you successfully stage a Christmas bazaar, you might be hooked on the idea of weekend entrepreneuring and venture into a year-round business. Read more about it in Chapter 5, "Crafty Business."

6. Foraging the wild for profit. Foraging in the wild for supplies to use in crafts projects or for wild items to market is a terrific enterprise for the whole family! You can even turn an afternoon's outing into a geology lesson, history lesson, or nature hike while at the same time picking up things that will turn into cash later on. Read more about foraging in Chapter 3, "Old-Fashioned Money."

7. Niche newsletter. Housewife Amy Dacyczyn made the decision to stay home with her children and earn extra money by publishing *The Tightwad Gazette*. With national exposure for her newsletter and a bestselling book, she has exceeded her wildest dreams. Small newsletters are cropping up to serve the interests of many different groups, from snowboarders to fans of singalong karaoke bars. Target the right audience, and your niche newsletter could bring money in the mail every day! Learn more about newsletter publishing in Chapter 9, "Long Shots."

8. Custom window coverings with matching bedspreads. With a flair for design and a skill for sewing, you can cash in on the craze for custom window treatments. Sew window coverings from beautiful fabrics your customers have purchased and make matching bedspreads while working at your own pace in an extra room in your house. A large part of the demand for custom curtains and bedspreads is for nurseries and children's rooms. Chapter 5, "Crafty Business," has a complete description.

9. Potpourri and herbal products. What better way to enjoy your own beautiful garden than to fill it with roses, lavender, and culinary herbs to turn into high-priced retail products you can market at fairs and local stores? Read how Darcy Teitjen has prospered with her potpourri business and how you can start one too. See Chapter 5, "Crafty Business," for more information.

10. **Prop rental.**   Find out how you can earn extra money by renting your antique furniture, collectible china, heirloom silver, and other items to photographers and food stylists. The beauty of the prop rental business is that you can rent out the same things over and over, making money each time! Read about Mimi Luebbermann's success in Chapter 6, "Odds and Ends."

These are just the top ten businesses for moms at home. Once you decide how much time you are willing to devote to a weekend (or spare-time) business, you should read through all of the ideas outlined in this book. The perfect idea just might catch your eye, and you will be on your way to the bank in no time at all!

Index

Books for Entrepreneurs
from Prima Publishing

Mail-Order Success Secrets
by Tyler Hicks $12.95
Is owning your own business your goal? Then mail order is
the low-cost, high-profit way to go. Among the areas covered:
how to start your business, where to find your product, how to
get low-cost publicity, the overseas' mail-order market, tapping
into the 800-number boom, and more.

199 Great Home Businesses You Can Start (and Succeed in!)
for Under $1,000
by Tyler Hicks $12.95
Helps you classify the type of business that would best suit
you—People, Non-People, Stay-at-Home, or Go-Outside—and
then offers dozens of possible businesses you can build. From
gift baskets to seminar promotion, personal shopping services
to medical claims processing, Hicks has the right business
for you.

Pay Dirt: How to Raise and Sell Herbs and Produce for
SERIOUS CA$H
by Mimi Leubbermann $12.95
Explains everything a prospective small-time farmer needs to
know—from what to grow and how to grow it to how and
where to sell it. Almost any backyard or apartment porch is
big enough for some of these simple, home-based businesses.

The Complete Work-at-Home Companion
by Herman Holtz $14.95
Offers advice on setting up the ideal work situation for those
estimated 14 million people who work from the home, both
part-time and full-time. Holtz offers clear advice on setting up
the ideal office as well as getting maximum mileage from computer hardware and software. Learn how to overcome distrac-
tions, price your products, handle taxes and insurance, and
much more.

FILL IN AND MAIL TODAY

PRIMA PUBLISHING
P.O. BOX 1260BK
ROCKLIN, CA 95677

USE YOUR VISA/MC AND ORDER BY PHONE:
(916) 786-0426 (Mon–Fri 9–4 p.m. PST)

Dear People at Prima,
Please send me the following titles:

Quantity	Title	Amount
_____	_____	_____
_____	_____	_____
_____	_____	_____
_____	_____	_____
_____	_____	_____

	Subtotal	$_____
	Postage & Handling	$___3.95___
	7.25% Sales Tax (California only)	$_____
	TOTAL (U.S. funds only)	$_____

☐ Check enclosed for $_____ (payable to Prima Publishing)

Charge my   ☐ MasterCard   ☐ Visa

Account No. _____ Exp. Date _____

Signature _____

Your Name _____

Address _____

City/State/Zip _____

Daytime Telephone (   ) _____

YOU MUST BE SATISFIED, OR YOUR MONEY BACK!!!
Thank You for Your Order